Enough's Enough

(And Other Rules of Life)

BOOKS BY CALVIN TRILLIN

AN EDUCATION IN GEORGIA

BARNETT FRUMMER IS AN
UNBLOOMED FLOWER

U.S. JOURNAL

AMERICAN FRIED

RUNESTRUCK

ALICE, LET'S EAT

FLOATER

UNCIVIL LIBERTIES

THIRD HELPINGS

KILLINGS

WITH ALL DISRESPECT

IF YOU CAN'T SAY SOMETHING NICE

TRAVELS WITH ALICE

ENOUGH'S ENOUGH
(AND OTHER RULES OF LIFE)

Enough's Enough

(And Other Rules of Life)

Calvin Trillin

Ticknor & Fields · New York · 1990

For information about permission to reproduce selections from
this book, write to Permissions, Ticknor & Fields,
215 Park Avenue South, New York, New York 10003.

Library of Congress Cataloging-in-Publication Data
Trillin, Calvin.
Enough's enough (and other rules of life) / Calvin Trillin.
p. cm.
A collection of the author's columns, 1987–1990.
ISBN 0-89919-958-5
1. United States — Politics and government — 1981–1989 — Humor.
2. United States — Social life and customs — 1971– — Humor.
I. Title.
E876.T749 1990 90-36205
973.927'0207 — dc20 CIP

Printed in the United States of America

AGM 10 9 8 7 6 5 4 3 2 1

The columns in this book were originally distributed for
publication through King Features Syndicate. Some of them have
been altered, merged, or taken out of chronological order.

To the correctly named Calvin Comfort,
and all the other Comforts — Ruthie,
Anna, Judy, and Alan

Contents

Contents

Enough's Enough

(And Other Rules of Life)

Foreword

OCCASIONALLY, I MEET someone whose response to learning that I write a newspaper column is to ask for what is sometimes called advice to the lovelorn — what to do, for instance, about the fact that his wife comes in hours after the bowling alley has closed for the evening, flicks paper clips at him with a rubber band when he asks her where she's been, and always addresses him in front of important business contacts as "Sweet Potato."

"Pull up your socks," I tell him.

Looking somewhat puzzled, he might then try asking for a little advice on rearing children.

"Try to get one that doesn't spit up," I say. "Otherwise, you're on your own."

Around that time, my new acquaintance — we can call him Norbert — may turn to the sort of question that is usually answered with something like "Just rub the damaged porcelain with ordinary lemon juice, let it stand overnight, and then wipe with a clean, dry cloth." It's not usually answered that way by me, of course. The closest I've come to offering any household hints was a column expressing my confidence that many loyal readers would come forward with useful ideas for my friend

Jane, who had some rather persuasive evidence that there were cockroaches in her computer. When it turned out that my confidence was misplaced, I abandoned the genre.

As long as I'm at it, I might as well admit that I may have also had a fling or two at child-rearing advice — mainly columns discussing every American father's solemn duty to persuade his children that when he was a child he had to walk barefoot ten miles through the snow just to get to school.

It was a column about child rearing, in fact, that led to the title for this book. The column concerned a friend of ours, a widow who, in addition to holding down a full-time job, was in the often entertaining but occasionally nerve-racking position of trying to raise a son — Nick, by name — who was what my mother would have called a handful. When Nick was seven or eight, his mother finally decided that she should post some explicit rules on the refrigerator door so that he'd know where he stood — although, as far as I could see, Nick knew perfectly well where he stood, which was often on the dining room table in dirty sneakers. Rule Number Six was "Enough's enough."

Nick is in college now, but to this day I often begin conversations with him by saying, "Rule Number Six, Nick" — a custom that one of the child-rearing-advice columnists might put in the category of preventive strikes. Maybe because Rule Number Six became such a strong element in our local folklore, we all gradually forgot the other rules. Then, a few years ago, Nick suddenly remembered Rule Number One: "Tone of voice." A lot of people don't think a phrase like "Tone of voice" can be a rule; most rules would include a verb, for instance. People who don't think "Tone of voice" can be a rule are people who don't have any children.

Not long after Nick remembered "Tone of voice," I read in the paper about a bank robbery in Brooklyn, an amateurish job that netted the robber a couple of thousand dollars. As the robber ran out of the bank, the bank manager, a woman in her middle years, ran out after him, chased him down the street, tackled him, and was apparently in danger of doing him some serious physical damage when she was restrained by a couple of passing sanitation men. When she was asked why she had responded to the robbery so aggressively, she said that the bank had been robbed the previous year and "Enough's enough."

Of course, the unfortunate robber had no idea that the bank manager felt that way. If he had, he might have tried another bank. In fairness to the robber, there should have been a sign at the bank — posted where banks keep those signs listing all the reasons they have for not cashing your check — that said RULE NUMBER SIX STRICTLY ENFORCED AT THIS BRANCH. Reading about the bank robbery made me realize that we'd all be better off if Rule Number Six were more widely posted on refrigerator doors. That is particularly true when it comes to refrigerator doors in Washington, D.C.

Not knowing any of this, Norbert waits in awkward silence for some advice on how to restore stained table linens. Then my wife walks over and, acknowledging me with a jerk of the head, says something to Norbert like, "If he did household hints, a lot of households would be in serious trouble."

"Then what exactly does he do?" Norbert asks. By this time, I am standing silently off to the side as if I were a somewhat odd-looking beast being categorized by a couple of dog walkers ("The people who sold him to us said he was pure Golden Retriever, but we think there's some Lab in there somewhere").

"He does, well, sort of, commentary," my wife says.

Norbert brightens up. "I read somewhere that in this country we spend $520,720 a minute on defense," he says to me. "What does that mean?"

"Well," I say, "that means that if you take the amount of money we spend annually on defense and divide it by the number of minutes in a year, you'd come out with $520,720."

Norbert stares at me for a while. "Well, I knew that," he finally says, sounding a little put out. "But what does it mean? What's the significance?"

"Beats the hell out of me," I say.

My wife steps in and starts describing me to Norbert again. I'm back in my Golden Retriever mode. "I'm afraid he doesn't do significance," she says.

Norbert turns to me, looking, I must say, rather hostile. "Are you one of those columnists who's always writing about how funny it was the time the basement got flooded during Christmas dinner?"

"We don't have floods in our basement," I said. "There just isn't any room left down there. On the other hand, maybe there is a flood in our basement and with all the other stuff around it's just hard to tell."

Norbert turns back to my wife. "What does your husband usually write about?" he asks.

At that point, my wife usually washes her hands of the matter and looks at me for a reply.

"Actually, what I do is make snide, underhanded, and often unfair remarks about public officials and other decent citizens," I say. "When I don't have a public official to cuff around, I'll admit, I dump the irritations of daily life on innocent readers I don't even know. If all else fails, I write about the trouble I'm having with my teeth."

"Aren't you ashamed of making a living that way?" he says.

"Well, I'll say just one thing in my defense," I tell him. "It's not much of a living."

Phone Pals

March 23, 1987

"I'M TELEPHONING, sir, to inform you that you have been preselected by computer to win a trip to Hawaii for only $1,198, including air travel and hotel room — that's double occupancy — and a free Mahu Lahani cocktail upon arrival."

"How nice of you to call! As I was just saying to a gentleman who phoned to tell me I'd been chosen as someone who could benefit greatly from a cattle-ranch mutual fund, it's always comforting to hear the telephone ring around dinnertime and know that people with a large computer at their disposal have been thinking of me."

"Then I take it, sir, that you'd like to redeem your exclusive, limited-time offer to take advantage of this special award?"

"And you'll be interested to hear that, by coincidence, my Uncle Harry has this weird obsession about visiting places that end with the letter *i*. I'll admit that the young woman who phoned last night to tell me that I had been selected for a specially priced series of tango lessons didn't seem absolutely entranced by Uncle Harry's travel theories, but then, she wasn't in the trade the way you are. You see, Uncle Harry's from Missouri, and he got the idea that it would be appropriate to visit any place whose name ends similarly."

"Sir, if I could just get your decision on this, you can charge it conveniently on your MasterCard or —"

"Oh, there were some he collected right away, of course. He and Aunt Rosie drove through Bemidji, Minnesota, one summer on the way to the lakes up there. And it wasn't long before he managed to score what he called his first double: Biloxi, Mississippi. It's on the Gulf Coast — but I guess you knew that, being in the travel business. Although, you'd be surprised: the man who phoned the other night to tell me I'd been preselected for eight days and seven nights in Cancun had never heard of Biloxi."

"This offer is for Hawaii, sir, and it includes —"

"Biloxi's just down the coast from Gulfport, which has a lovely motto: 'Where Your Ship Comes In.' "

"Sir, Hawaii is a land of enchantment, where many cultures have —"

"You might say I collect mottos, the way my Uncle Harry collects places that end in *i*. Do you collect anything yourself?"

"Uh. Well. Actually, I do have a lot of poodle-dog ornaments. But about this Hawaiian trip, sir —"

"Underrated dog, the poodle, and I suppose that goes for the ornaments too. But you didn't phone to discuss poodle dogs. Listen, my Aunt Rosie, who considers Biloxi just about far enough from home, called all worried one day to say that Uncle Harry was talking about the two of them going to Africa so he could visit Mali. Well, I told her that Uncle Harry just likes to talk about the more exotic places — Haiti, say, or Bari, Italy, or Lodi, New Jersey. So she didn't have to worry about dragging herself all the way over to Bamako. That's the capital of

Mali, by the way: Bamako. I had a friend who was sent there by the foreign service. I remember at the going-away party somebody sang a song called 'I'll Be Your Bamako Baby, You Be My Mali Dolly.' It must be interesting doing what you do — calling people around dinnertime and finding out capitals of foreign countries that happen to end in *i*."

"Sir, when I say this offer is a limited-time offer, I really have to —"

"I know: you really have to get to the point. Of course. I can see that. The point is this: Uncle Harry has always talked about going to Hawaii, a one-word double. He figured that even if he didn't get to Tahiti and Fiji and Funafuti while he was out that way, he might spend his time in Hawaii in the town of Kahului on the island of Maui. I think if he did that, Uncle Harry would be a happy man. Although I have to say that Aunt Rosie disagrees with me. She says that no matter where he went, Uncle Harry would be a stubborn, mean-tempered old coot. Of course, Aunt Rosie —"

"Sir! Sir!"

"Yes?"

"Maybe your Uncle Harry would like to take advantage of this limited-time offer for a trip to Hawaii."

"But Uncle Harry hasn't been preselected by computer. I'm the one who's been preselected by computer."

"Well, I think just this once . . ."

"Oh, he would never be party to anything like that. I guess I've told you before what Aunt Rosie always says about Uncle Harry being as flexible as a tree stump. Take his theory that Christopher Columbus's first New World landing was in Kansas City, near what is now the corner of Eleventh and Walnut. Why, he . . . Hello? . . . Hello? . . ."

Of an Age

April 27, 1987

I'M NOT SURE I'm ready for the notion that there's something chic about Australia. Remember when Australia was a synonym for boredom? Oh. Maybe you don't. Maybe you're twenty-eight. Maybe my problem is that I remember too much. It may be that the world sometimes seems topsy-turvy to me because I remember it when it was turvy-topsy.

This winter, there seemed to be a lot of discussions on television about how someone's reasoning process changes over the years — the real subject being whether or not President Reagan was, to put it as respectfully as possible, operating on a full battery pack. I'm not as old as the President, but I'm long enough in the tooth to know something about growing older that none of the experts on TV mentioned: the reason the world seems more and more disorienting as you grow older is not because there's anything wrong with your mind but because you're in a better and better position to understand how disoriented the world is.

Take the notion that Australia now carries great cachet when it comes to motion pictures and yachting and fashion and, for all

I know, perfume. That notion may be accepted routinely by someone too young to know otherwise. He may very well swallow the same stuff about New Zealand next.

But how about someone old enough to remember that for decades Australia was spoken of in a kindly way only by elderly American tourists who treasured it as the farthest-away clean place where people spoke English? How about someone who managed to go for thirty years without mentioning Australia at all unless he happened to fall into a conversation about relative per capita beer consumption among postindustrial nations? When that person reads in the paper that an Australian motif is now considered effective in pitching, say, exotic silk undergarments, he may be startled enough to blurt out, "You've got to be kidding!" If he happens to be on a crowded bus at the time, his fellow passengers look up and smile in a patronizing way, as if to say that the old codger is not operating on a full battery pack. A lot of bus passengers are twenty-eight.

People who are twenty-eight don't know enough to be confused. They may simply take it for granted, for instance, that the capital of China is a place called Beijing, and always has been. (You'll notice that nobody on the bus is reading a history book.) But how about the person of respectable age who spent twenty years under the impression that the capital of China — the very same Chinese city with the very same Chinese name — was a place called Peking?

Some years ago, when people who are now twenty-eight weren't old enough to use a newspaper for anything other than soaking it in flour and water and fashioning it into elephants, grown-ups were informed by their newspapers one morning that the Chinese government had decided, after all these years, that the best English approximation of the Chinese name for the capital of China was not "Peking" after all but "Beijing." It's as if the American government had announced, rather casually, that upon reflection it had been decided that the capital of the United States should be pronounced not as if it were spelled "Washington" but as if it were spelled "Rumington."

That news from China would have been stupefying enough under any conditions. It came, though, not that long after a period when the American Secretary of State was not even referring to Peking as Peking. He still called it Peiping, because the suffix "king" in Chinese — which he didn't even realize was actually the suffix "jing" — means capital, and our government didn't recognize Peking as the capital. Why? Because our government didn't acknowledge the existence of China, and a place that doesn't exist obviously can't have a capital — particularly if it happens to be the sort of place that couldn't make up its mind how to pronounce a capital if it had one.

So a bus passenger of respectable age who hears the people across the aisle rave about the touring acrobats from Beijing — a place he has heard called two other things for twenty or thirty years while it was the capital of a country his government said did not exist — should be able to say "From where?" without the twenty-eight-year-old person behind him saying something like, "Whatsamatter, pops, elevator service not going all the way to the top floor these days?"

If that same respectably aged bus passenger turns to his morning paper and reads an advertisement about "spring fashions direct from Melbourne," he may well say out loud, "You've got to be kidding!" But that doesn't mean he's dotty. It means that the world is dotty. Don't you see? Maybe you don't. Maybe you're twenty-eight.

Telling All

May 4, 1987

THE SENATORS WHO THINK we have to tear down the new American Embassy in Moscow just because it's full of bugging devices have apparently never heard of the drone effect. It's a scientific phenomenon that I can explain in one sentence: The more someone has to listen to, the less he hears.

The breakthrough work on the drone effect was done during the Second World War by psychological researchers in the United States Army, working with Troop Information and Education lectures. The longer the lecture that soldiers were subjected to on personal hygiene, it was discovered, the dirtier they got.

Those who understand the principle of the drone effect understand that tearing down the embassy is the opposite of what we should do in Moscow. The point is not to keep the Russians from overhearing anything but to force them to listen to absolutely everything.

I'm not talking about the bore bomb here. The bore bomb's different. I revealed the existence of the Russian bore bomb strategy back in 1974, although I didn't use the term then because it was still classified. At the time of my discovery, I was going through the Russian exhibition at a world's fair in Spokane, peering at displays that thoroughly described, say, "an installation for gasification of highly sulfurous black oil." Suddenly I realized what should have been apparent years ago from those stories about how American Communists used to take over organizations in the thirties by giving long speeches until everyone else got tired of waiting for the vote and went home: the Communists have long been engaged in a conspiracy to bore the world into submission.

When I read that the KGB had planted bimbo-spies to seduce Marine guards at our embassy in Moscow, I realized that the bimbo-spies were probably equipped with bore bombs. I see a Marine saying to some sexy KGB colonel who has been working at the embassy as an astonishingly voluptuous window washer, "Ma'am, if you'd just promise not to say one more word about the Siberia-Krasnoyark hydroelectric power station at Divnogorsk, you can have your way with me."

Getting into a bore bomb race with the Russians would be futile. Even with the Senate on our side, we'd never catch up. A year or so ago, at the twenty-seventh congress of the Communist Party, Mikhail Gorbachev gave a speech that lasted one entire day. This was a speech to his own supporters. Imagine the sort of damage he could inflict on an enemy!

The drone effect is a completely different piece of strategy. The way it works is this: We give absolutely everything the same security classification — Top Secret — and we send it all everywhere. Then we let the Russians worry about picking out the good stuff.

For instance, I read somewhere that the new trade bill is something like nine hundred eighty-nine pages long. We should send a copy of it to the American Embassy in Moscow, in a package that is marked in large letters TOP SECRET. The way I envision this, KGB translators begin poring over the bill, figuring that instructions from the State Department on medium-range missile policy are in there somewhere. Before they get halfway through it, though, some bimbo spy winks at a Marine guard and is given an eight-hundred-page Department of Agriculture report entitled "Farm Price Supports: A Thirty-Year Overview, Concentrating on But Not Exclusive to Soybean Pricing Structures." The KGB puts all translators on overtime.

Meanwhile, all packages to the American Embassy in Moscow are marked in large letters TOP SECRET. The KGB is reading everything, having no way of knowing where it might run across the NATO contingency battle plans for northern Europe — which happen to have been written into the Tax Reform Act of 1986, somewhere after page five hundred.

The best English translators in the KGB are getting glassy-eyed, and there's no end in sight. A junior clerk in the American Embassy is reading the *Congressional Record* into the bug that is assumed to be in the downstairs powder room. Long memos that explain supply-side economics are being placed in an area accessible to the cook, who is known to leave each night with every document she can lay her hands on, along with most of the rump roast.

The Russians are buried in information. There are long lines in the shops because so many workers have had to be diverted from the manufacturer of consumer goods to read lists of Republican campaign donors and make transcripts of Top Secret speeches by congressmen on the reasons we celebrate Mother's Day. Our embassy is secure, although the document glut has made it overcrowded. The State Department decides to build another new embassy. The Russians ask if we'd be terribly hurt if they didn't bug it.

Pen Pals

April 6, 1987

SOME TIME AGO, I mentioned that those little subscription cards that are always falling out of magazines can be used to write encouraging notes to the magazine's employees. The way I figured it, working in the department that processes the cards — what magazines call Circulation Fulfillment — can't be much fun. There's the frustration involved in trying to decipher a lot of bad handwriting. There's the constant threat of paper cuts. There's the nagging feeling that the true romance of working for, say, *Newsweek* may be connected with being a foreign correspondent in Paris rather than with being a card sorter in Livingston, New Jersey. It was my simple notion that if the magazine is thoughtful enough to provide the postage — almost all of the cards say right on them "No Postage Necessary If Mailed in the United States" — the least we can do is to write "Keep up the good work, Circulation Fulfillment people" on the card and drop it in the mail. There's no need to subscribe.

I hope the Circulation Fulfillment people aren't growing tired of getting the same message again and again. Just in case, I've branched out a bit lately. For a while I varied the messages, alternating "Keep up the good work, Circulation Fulfillment people" with "Circulation Fulfillment is the heart of the operation" and "Foreign correspondents often have problems getting their laundry done."

Then I realized that Circulation Fulfillment people would probably be happier receiving messages that seem tailored more to them personally. We all like to feel special. The next time I was on an airplane that furnished an array of magazines, I gathered the cards from *Time* and *Life* and *People* and *Sports Illustrated*, all of which are addressed to Chicago, and sent them in with messages like "A woolly scarf will do wonders against that wind coming off the lake" or "It's a real shame about those Sox."

"Did you know you're not the only Circulation Fulfillment person in Boulder, Colorado?" I wrote on a *U.S. News* card to someone I pictured as a middle-aged gentleman who works in a business suit and has a penchant for expressing himself in graphs. "There's someone from *Vogue* in your very same zip code. You might consider her a bit snooty at first, and her first impression of you might be that you're a little, well, boring, but I think you two could learn a lot from each other. P.S. My sister, Sukey, went to the University of Colorado."

I like to think that all of the Circulation Fulfillment people in Boulder have gotten to know each other now. I often envision them gathering after work in a tasteful gazebo behind the *House & Garden* building. They trade eyestrain stories and talk about whether the *Esquire* men among them will really be able to arrange for an article called "Fifty Circulation Fulfillment People Under Thirty-five Who Are Changing America."

Sooner or later, I decided that it wasn't fair to limit my words of encouragement to Circulation Fulfillment people. On a card that dropped out of a *GQ* (formerly *Gentlemen's Quarterly*) while I was trying to find out if it's considered O.K. to wear a Tonganoxie High School sweatshirt to a garden party, I wrote to the Franklin Mint to say, "I don't actually have a strong need for a proof set of 'The Treasure Coins of the Caribbean' right at this time, but keep up the good work." On a card I found in *The New Yorker*, I tossed off an encouraging message to the Lindblad people, who lead nature tours to places like the Galapagos Islands: "Travel is broadening."

Then I discovered those full-page Visa applications that are designed to be torn out of the magazine, folded over, and sealed. At last I had a postage-paid way to return a lot of things I hadn't asked for in the first place — for instance, the ads that I've had to tear off the return envelope every month before I could send my check in to the Visa folks. Fortunately, I had held on to all of those ads — I figured there was always a chance I'd get a sudden craving for, say, a carry-on bag that unfolds into a clock radio — and I was able to stuff a three-year supply of them into an application for the Chase Manhattan Visa Premier World Card which I found stitched into an issue of *The Atlantic*. I included a short but courteous message: "Thanks anyway."

I realize that not everybody has the time to do all that folding and stuffing. I've been delighted to hear that some busy people now drop every subscription card into the mail even if they don't have time to write any message at all, just to let some Circulation Fulfillment person know he's not forgotten. To those busy people, and to everyone who's responded to my suggestion, I just want to say, "Keep up the good work."

Thoughts of Females in the Spring, Tra-La

May 11, 1987

I KNOW I'M GOING to get in trouble for this. I'm supposed to believe that the reason men tend to have more interest in, say, carburetors than women do is because little boys are given trucks at Christmas instead of dolls. I do believe that. Really. I've believed it for years. I continued to believe it even after my friend Bernie Mohler, the feminist, gave his five-year-old daughter a catcher's mitt for Christmas only to have her plant a marigold in it.

I believe all that stuff. I've even cooperated to the extent of maintaining total ignorance when it comes to carburetors. I'm not absolutely sure what a carburetor looks like, but, given the choice, I'm certain I'd rather have a doll. I'm just fine on this issue. Except for this: I believe that in the spring female human beings get a deep biological urge to replace the living room slipcovers.

I'm not talking about something imposed by society, something that has to do with getting dollhouses for Christmas. I'm talking about something buried way down there in the chromosomes somewhere. And I'm talking about all women. I believe that in the spring Margaret Thatcher, on her way out of 10 Downing Street to deliver a stiff lecture to a group of poor people, will stop as she strides through the living room, turn to the Chancellor of the Exchequer, and say, "Doesn't it seem to you that the chintz on that armchair by the window is getting a bit tatty?" I believe that Sandra Day O'Connor's thoughts turn to slipcovers in the spring. So do the thoughts of female automobile mechanics and female physicists and female mud wrestlers. So, as it happens, do the thoughts of my wife.

Come springtime, I find her in the living room, staring hard at the couch. "How long have we had that couch?" she asks. That's an indication that her plans for the couch go beyond new slipcovers. When it comes to furniture, I try not to get into a discussion with my wife about length of service, because on that subject our figures tend to differ. She'll fix her glance on some innocent armchair that I think of as brand-new, and say, "Well, we've had almost forty years of good wear out of that armchair now . . ."

She thinks the resistance I have every spring to replacing the couch is caused by stinginess. She's wrong. Only part of it is caused by stinginess. I've never denied that I have had trouble accepting the contemporary assumption that painting a wall will cost more than the wall cost in the first place. But there's also a factor that has nothing to do with stinginess. It's biological. Take the conversation we had just last week:

"What do you think of that couch?" my wife asked.

"Couch?" I said. "What about the couch?" This is an answer that is preselected by a biological code.

"What do you see when you look at that couch?" my wife asked.

"See?" I said."Couch? Which couch are we talking about?"

"There's only one couch," she said.

"Oh, that one," I said. "Well, I see a piece of furniture with a back and cushions and four stubby little legs. I see a sitting instrument. I see a device designed to hold human beings, once they've folded themselves in two places."

"You don't see how threadbare it's getting on the arms?"

"Arms?" I said. "Threadbare?" (You can tell that these answers are biologically mandated: nobody would sound that dumb if he had a choice in the matter.)

"I don't think you do see it," she said. "I honestly don't think you can see it."

"Making fun of someone's physical handicaps is the last thing I expected from you," I said. I wasn't talking about my eyesight. I was talking about my biologically imposed inability to see the need for a new piece of furniture as soon as my wife saw it.

"Maybe we can just make do with new slipcovers instead of getting a whole new couch," she said.

"Well, I agree that this is probably not the best time to buy a new couch," I said, jumping at the opportunity to encourage the less damaging of two serious hits. "Particularly considering the money we're probably going to have to spend on the car."

"The car?" she asked. "What's wrong with the car?"

"Well, I haven't had it looked at yet," I said, "but I don't like the way the carburetor's sounding."

Scandal Glut

June 1, 1987

WE'VE GOT OURSELVES a scandal glut. That's right. I didn't want to say this. I was hoping to get away with calling it a slight oversupply. I can't. It's a glut. We're awash in scandal. It's coming up over the curbs. We've got scandal in the White House and scandal on Wall Street and scandal in the ministry and scandal in the presidential campaign and scandal in the Southwestern Conference. On the television networks, we've got afternoons full of dingbat foreign-affairs cowboys testifying about how they tried to subvert the government and chew gum at the same time, then evenings full of preachers accusing each other of stuff that's supposed to be available only on cable. We've got a situation where an investigation by special counsel of the attorney general of the United States over allegations of plain old-fashioned graft can hardly make the papers. That's no oversupply. That's a glut.

Look at what happened to former Secretary of Labor Raymond Donovan, the first Cabinet secretary in the history of the United States to be indicted while in office, who was just found not guilty after an eight-month trial in the Bronx. Donovan has said he was treated unfairly, and he's right: the customary stance for a public official to take when he finds himself on trial is to point at the pack of jostling TV cameramen and pushy scribblers who are following him down the corridor of the courthouse and shout, "You people brought this on! You hound every decent man out of office!" But for most of the eight months, there wasn't anyone there for him to shout at. Because of the scandal glut, reporters just couldn't make it to all the trials, so they skipped some of the trials in the outer boroughs.

Maybe the guy who covers the Bronx courts part-time for one of the neighborhood papers dropped in now and then to doze in the back row. But how can you claim to be hounded by one guy who's not even fully awake? When Donovan was acquitted, he had to settle for charging that the Bronx district attorney had done it all for the publicity, but that sounded pretty lame: the D.A. could obviously have gotten more coverage dedicating a new ramp at the senior citizens' softball field.

It's getting to be too much. Until *Time* ran head shots of an assortment of Reagan Administration malefactors — a layout so extensive that it looked like one of those ads life insurance companies take to show you the faces of all salesmen in the tri-state area who have fobbed off more than a million dollars' worth of life insurance on an unsuspecting public — I hadn't even realized that people like the chief administrator of NASA and the chief of the Federal Aviation Authority had resigned under a cloud before I managed to learn their names. *Time* reported that more than a hundred members of the Reagan Administration have had ethical or legal charges leveled against them, and that doesn't include the people accused of flat-out dumbness.

I realize that you thought I liked scandals. You thought I was one of those press jackals who get their kicks from the troubles of their betters. You were right. But a glut causes complications even for us jackals. For instance, those of us who specialize in mean and underhanded remarks about public officials have to count on the public's having a certain familiarity with the latest thing the official has stolen or the latest bimbo he's been caught with. If you were the sort of person who wanted to make a joke — in the worst possible taste, of course — about Donna Rice, late of the Gary Hart campaign, you'd need to assume that your readers remember for sure who she is. These days, people are so overloaded with scandal information that by now they may think that Donna Rice is a code name for one of the *contra* cargo planes or the name of a deputy undersecretary forced to resign in a travel-voucher scam or the name of a grain company whose takeover was wired by the inside-trading crooks or the name some evangelical minister preferred to be called whenever he was in drag.

What worries me about all of this is that we may have a complete reversal of what people think of as news. If the investigation of the attorney general doesn't cause a ripple, people must simply assume that just every place is riddled with scandal. Then only the absence of scandal will be news. I can see a time when the only headlines that people find shocking are headlines like ENTIRE MATHEMATICS DEPARTMENT AT OKLAHOMA SOUTHERN UNIVERSITY FOUND SCANDAL-FREE or MOST METHODIST BISHOPS ARE NOT CROOKS. It will be a sad day for us jackals.

The Tip of the Iceberg

June 8, 1987

I SUPPOSE YOU'VE HEARD the news about what some Norwegian oceanographers just discovered: it turns out that the tip of an iceberg — what you see sticking out of the water — is the entire iceberg after all. You hadn't heard about that? Well, it's something for you to think about, particularly if you're one of those people who go around saying "It's just the tip of the iceberg" all the time.

I don't know about you, but I was always told that maybe as much as ninety percent of an iceberg was under water, completely out of sight. Otherwise I would never have said "It's just the tip of the iceberg" when I meant that whatever was immediately apparent was just a tiny part of what was going on. Of course, you may not feel that way at all. You may be one of those people who kept using the phrase "happy as a clam" even after that team of French marine biologists proved that the clam is, in fact, the most melancholy of bivalves. Some people are like that.

You didn't know about the clam research? Well, it happened several years ago. Some French marine biologists discovered that over many thousands of years clams, which of course don't possess the ability to reason the way higher forms do, have had built into their instinctual mechanism a deep desire to be scallops. No, I don't know how the French found that out. Scientists can do wonders these days.

Which brings up the question of why we didn't know years ago that the tip of an iceberg is just about all an iceberg amounts to. That was one of the first questions asked, of course, at the press conference called to announce this discovery, and I don't think the head of the Norwegian underwater exploration team, Lars Kulleseid, answered it satisfactorily when he replied, "You think you're such a big shot, you try going down there and freezing your caboose off!"

I also thought it was totally inappropriate for him to explain the principle of iceberg flotation by pointing to the ice cubes floating in a gin and tonic he drank throughout the briefing. I might point out, while we're at it, that about ninety percent of every ice cube he pointed to was below the surface — raising the possibility that Kulleseid doesn't know what he's talking about.

But why should he care? It happens that "just the tip of the iceberg" is a phrase that doesn't exist in Norwegian, except as applied to iceberg lettuce. (There is, of course, no tip on a head of iceberg lettuce. When the Norwegians say "just the tip of the iceberg lettuce," they mean it ironically — or as ironically as Norwegians mean anything — and whoever hears it usually falls to the ground in helpless laughter.) If Norwegians want to get across the thought that we express with the phrase "just the tip of the iceberg," they say "just the snoot of the hen." I can't imagine why.

People who speak English, though, now have to consider

abandoning the iceberg metaphor completely or changing its meaning. If we're going to be absolutely accurate, after all, "the tip of the iceberg" now means exactly the same thing as "the whole kit and caboodle" — or would mean exactly the same thing if that team of historians from the University of Edinburgh hadn't discovered that it was almost impossible in the old days to find a whole caboodle, considering how fragile they were.

This is most disruptive. I suppose you remember what happened when those Canadian zoologists finally discovered that bats can actually see rather well, forcing everybody to decide what to do about the phrase "blind as a bat." Maybe you were out of the country then. Anyway, the zoologists said the one animal that was truly blind was the cave shrimp. I don't know about you, but I didn't begin to go around saying, "Without my glasses, I'm as blind as a cave shrimp." It just didn't sound right.

So I'm not sure I'm going to go along with this one either. Maybe if we all agree to ignore it, everyone will forget what's literally, scientifically true about icebergs, the way just about everyone forgot about that research showing that the thin edge of the wedge doesn't really open the way for a lot more to follow, because the thin edge usually breaks off. After all, it may be that there are all sorts of research projects ruinous to metaphors going on and this iceberg business just happens to be the only one we know about. I was about to say that this may be just the tip of the iceberg, except that "tip of the iceberg" doesn't mean "tip of the iceberg" anymore. Maybe.

Under the Hood

July 6, 1987

THE NEW LAW that permits states to raise their speed limit to sixty-five miles an hour is presumably not going to have much effect on the advertising strategy of the folks who manufacture Porsches: the top speed they've been advertising for their 928S 4 model is still a hundred miles per hour over the highest speed a car is legally permitted to travel in this country.

The Audi television commercial I've seen doesn't mention top speed. It simply shows an Audi driving at what I calculate at ninety or so along a track that looks like a toy my kids used to have that was called the Super Dooper Double Looper. Along the bottom of the picture, there's a sort of disclaimer that says something like, "Professional driver shown. Do not attempt these maneuvers." I suspect it was written by the same copywriter who composed the famous bean-package warning that says, "Warning: Do Not Put Beans up Nose."

Someone who reads an advertisement claiming that the Mercedes can go 140 miles an hour or an advertisement that says the new Mazda RX-7 SE sports car has a top speed of 128 may draw the conclusion that it's now O.K. to advertise some of the illegal uses of consumer goods. You might get the idea that we're going to start to see sledgehammer ads that say "Excellent for knocking through bricks to enter warehouses late at night" or airplane glue ads that say "One good sniff will make you higher than the plane" or ski mask ads that say "Preferred by stick-up men of convenience stores everywhere."

I don't think that will happen. As we're always being told, after all, the automobile has a special place in American society. What other product, for instance, could get away with giving itself a name as silly as RX-7 SE? It sounds like something that an eight-year-old might send away for to run on his Super Dooper Double Looper. Can you imagine calling your washing machine that? ("I just got me one of those new GR-850 Panther stack models. Smooth. Real smooth.")

Also, American consumers have always had the same feeling about the capacity of their cars that Pentagon generals have about their supply of nuclear warheads: enough is definitely not enough. Any car that wants to appeal to an audience wider than aged and infirm Sunday-school teachers advertises how fast it can go from zero to sixty — presumably on the assumption that almost any American family would want a vehicle that can hold its own in a drag race, just in case.

The new Chevrolet Beretta, for instance, advertises "brand-new microprocessor technology to handle 600,000 commands per second." I can think of only about half a dozen commands I'd want to give a car; "start" and "stop" are the main ones. That may leave the Beretta owner with a command capacity that is somewhere around 599,994 more than he needs to drive the car — but just about exactly what he needs to talk about the car. Otherwise, he wouldn't be able to give his new Beretta a little pat on its right fender and say, "This baby here can take 600,000 commands a second," thus driving a stake through the heart of his competitive neighbor, whose new car can handle only 450,000 commands per second.

In other words, Americans have always bought what the Porsche ad describes as Professor Porsche's philosophy: "A car should do more than simply move people from one point to another." But no one would run an advertisement quoting, say, Professor Westinghouse as teaching that "a washing machine should do more than simply wash clothes." So the automobile remains a special case. There's no need to worry about the rules of advertising changing in general. I don't think we're going to be seeing toaster ads that say "Air-cooled engine with turbocharger and intercooler, capable of taking 40,000 bagel-toasting commands per microsecond."

On the other hand, I've been wrong before. Someday, that housewife I'm always seeing on washing machine commercials could stand there with a straight face next to her washing machine — a GR-850 Panther stack model — and say, "This baby has the capacity to wash the combat fatigues of a full regiment of Afghan regulars who've been a month in the field." Then she'll give it a little pat.

Naming the Baby

July 20, 1987

I HAD A DISCUSSION with a friend of mine named Ruthie, who's five, about what to name the baby her mother is expecting in the fall. If her parents would simply agree to name the baby Calvin, Ruthie and I wouldn't have to bother with all this, but I'm used to making do with a fallback position.

I thought I'd start by seeing what Ruthie would think of a movie star name. For all I know, after all, a family that spurns a dignified name like Calvin might have unspoken aspirations toward the Cinema III marquee.

"How about Tab?" I asked Ruthie.

"Well then, how about Diet Coke?" Ruthie said.

"I'll make the jokes here, kid," I said.

If Diet Coke was the kind of response I could expect from Ruthie, I realized, there was no use going on with movie star names. I had plenty of other ideas.

"What do you think of Nigel?" I asked Ruthie.

"Nigel is a yucky name," Ruthie said. "That's what I think."

The kid's a stone wall. Nigel happens to be one of the names I've been crusading for as part of a plan to further Anglo-American friendship. I've always thought that one reason the English resent Americans is that we've never been willing to use the boys' names they favor, and they've always suspected us of thinking that their names are for sissies. So here's my plan: For the next few years, a lot of Americans name their boys Nigel and Cedric and Cyril and Trevor and Simon, and we invite the English to name their boys American names — unless, of course, they'd rather name them Calvin. Then, sooner or later, the United States will have a lot of grown-up men with English-sounding names and there will be a lot of people in England named LeRoy and Sonny and Darrell.

Think of how proud the English would be on the first year that every single linebacker on the National Football League all-star team is named Nigel. If the plan works perfectly, the Queen's Honors List that same year will have on it a noted musicologist named Sir Darrell Thistlethwaite.

In fact, I'm about to start advocating the same kind of plan to draw the various regions of this country closer together. I divide the United States into only two regions myself — the part of the country that had major league baseball before the Second World War (the *ancien* United States) and the part that didn't (the Expansion Team United States). For people who are too young to know which is which, here's how to tell: if you go to an Italian restaurant and the waiter's name is Duane, you're in the Expansion Team United States. So now I'm encouraging Easterners as well as English people to name their babies Duane. If they go for Duane, we'll try Odie out on them.

"I don't suppose you'd be in favor of Duane, would you?" I asked Ruthie, whose family happens to be completely Eastern.

"I don't suppose you'd go jump in the lake," Ruthie said.

I could see that the baby was going to have a hard time living with this smart-aleck no matter what his name was. From what I could gather, Ruthie favored double-barreled names, but not the sort of normal double-barreled names that I was familiar with from being around the people in my high school — people like Dogbite Davis and Six-Pack Sawyer. For instance, she had the idea that a good name for the baby might be Static Cling.

"I never heard of a baby named Static Cling," I said.

"Well then, how about Freezer Burn?" Ruthie said.

I know Easterners who at that point would have run off to their psychiatrist to find out why both of Ruthie's suggestions for the new baby's name happened to be minor household irritations. Fortunately, though, I'm from the Midwest, where there are only a couple of psychiatrists, both of them friendly guys who wear plaid golf pants and are named Duane.

"I read that it's a mistake to give a baby a name that could be either a boy or a girl," I said to Ruthie. "So I guess that pretty much rules out both Freezer Burn and Static Cling, not to speak of Diet Coke."

"Diet Coke is a boy's name, silly," Ruthie said.

"I guess it is, now that you mention it," I said.

"So why are you just talking about boys' names?" she asked.

"You're right," I said. "Maybe it'll be a girl. I've got a pretty good girl's name: Ruthie."

"Somebody's already using that name," Ruthie said.

"Well, there aren't many Ruthies compared to how many Diet Cokes there are," I said.

"The baby's a boy," Ruthie said. "Definitely."

"Then we might as well call him Calvin," I said.

"Ugh," Ruthie said.

Good-Neighbor Policy

July 27, 1987

AMERICANS THINK OF Canada as the place where the cold fronts come down from. Canadians think of America as the place where the acid rain comes up from. This is called free trade.

To improve its image in the United States, Canada spends a lot of money running color advertisements in American magazines on subjects like how hip Toronto is. So you think nice thoughts about Canada all summer ("Boy, is that Toronto hip!"). Then in December some weatherman, standing in front of his map on the ten o'clock news, tells you that thanks to a front moving down from Canada, it's going to be cold enough tomorrow morning to freeze your socks to your feet. By spring, you're so irritated at Canadian cold fronts that the Canadian government has to spend more money on color advertisements about how good the fishing is in Newfoundland.

Obviously, what the Canadian government should do is take just a little bit of the money it's spending for magazine advertising and pay all of the TV weathermen not to mention Canada in connection with cold fronts, except, of course, in August. I'll bet that's what Mexico did. You don't think so? Then how do you explain the fact that you've never heard any television weathermen talk about a hot front moving up from Mexico? Get with it.

The Canadians probably think that paying off the weathermen would constitute a bribe. They should know better from close observation of the American government. When President Reagan said that he would never pay ransom for American hostages held in Lebanon and then investigators found that he had approved a plan in 1985 to pay a million dollars for each hostage, the White House said that the million dollars wasn't ransom because President Reagan said he would never pay ransom. In other words, all the Canadian government has to do is to announce that it never bribes anyone. Then it can pay off the weathermen. See how easy everything is?

The whole business about weather coming from someplace is silly anyway. You don't think so? Then tell me this: where does the weather start? I knew you wouldn't know. The answer happens to be La Porte, Indiana. You think that the weatherman there doesn't get up in front of his map on the ten o'clock news and talk about the high pressure system coming from somewhere else? Don't kid yourself.

Sure, there's another way to go: the Canadian government could take magazine ads saying that cold fronts come from Greenland. Why not? Show me a cold front that's come from Canada and I'll show you a cold front that could very well have been in Greenland the week before. It started in La Porte anyway.

The only other approach I see is for Canada to deny that there's any such thing as a cold front, which is more or less the approach to acid rain the Reagan Administration took for a few years. Then if the Canadian Prime Minister came to the United States some February and somebody from Buffalo or St. Paul said, "If there's no such thing as a cold front, how come my socks are frozen to my feet?" the Prime Minister would say, "Guards, arrest that man."

Finally, of course, the Reagan Administration decided that there was such a thing as acid rain. If there wasn't any such thing as acid rain, after all, what was it that Michael Deaver was taking a lot of money from the Canadian government to lobby for controls on? So you're thinking that by shoveling money in Deaver's direction the Canadians finally got as hip as they're always telling us Toronto is — right? Wrong. In the first place, Deaver got indicted. In the second place, it turns out that other people spent a lot more money than the Canadians did — more money than was spent on any other single lobbying effort last year, in fact — to block legislation that would control acid rain. And what was the name of the crowd lobbying against control of acid rain? It was called the Citizens for Sensible Control of Acid Rain. You didn't guess that? I'm not sure you've really been paying attention.

So the Canadians are back where they started from, after having forgotten a lesson of American politics that a child in Chicago would learn on his father's knee: "A responsible citizen never pays off the wrong alderman." Canada still gets blamed for the cold fronts. We're still sending acid rain their way just as fast as we can get it out of the smokestacks. Pretty soon, at least, they won't have to spend money to advertise the fishing in Newfoundland because there won't be any fish in Newfoundland. Meanwhile, I hope you've learned something.

Weighing Hummingbirds: A Primer

August 10, 1987

A HUMMINGBIRD WEIGHS as much as a quarter. I learned that early this summer while I was listening to a radio interview with a hummingbird expert on the Canadian Broadcasting Corporation. The CBC interviews interesting people just about all day long, at the same time that American stations are playing the sort of music that makes middle-aged people snap at their children.

I live in Canada in the summer, so by around Labor Day I know a lot of things like how a hummingbird compares in weight to small change. People who live in Canada year-round know even more than I do. What I know tends to drain away over the winter.

The other day, somebody called me in Canada from New York to ask what I thought about the fact that the number one and number two best sellers in the United States are books about how dumb Americans are. I said, "Hey, wait a minute! I know how much a hummingbird weighs. What's so dumb about that?" I did admit that I'd probably be forgetting whatever I knew about hummingbird weight by around February ("Let me see, was it thirty-five cents, or maybe half a buck?"). The person on the phone said that one of the books included a list of things Americans ought to be familiar with but aren't, and that hummingbird weight wasn't on it. Apparently the list runs more toward things like Planck's constant and the Edict of Nantes.

If the people who put together that list came up to Canada and asked a Canadian to identify the Edict of Nantes, the Canadian would just ask if he could answer at the end of the week, figuring that by then the CBC would have interviewed a Nantes specialist from the University of Western Ontario or somebody who just came back from a relief mission to Nantes or maybe the ambassador from Nantes to the United Nations, and the Edict would obviously have come up during the conversation. Once he got the Nantes question safely postponed, the Canadian would say to the list gatherers, "By the way, did you fellows know that a hummingbird weighs as much as a quarter?"

A Canadian quarter. As far as I know, bird weights mentioned on the CBC are always given in Canadian currency. For an American living in Canada, that was, of course, a question that came to mind right away. I find that facts learned from the CBC can start an entire chain of questions. For instance, the first thing I asked my wife about the hummingbird fact was this: Do you think a hummingbird also weighs the same as two dimes and a nickel?

Now that I think of it, that particular question didn't start a chain, because she said it was a stupid question and left it at that. But then she asked a question of her own: How do they weigh a hummingbird? Hummingbirds move around a lot, and my wife was concerned that someone who was intent on weighing one would have to do it in first.

"Not at all," I said, happy to be able to put her mind at ease on this question. "You've seen those TV documentaries where they shoot a dart into a panda to put him asleep long enough to outfit him with a radio transmitter. Well, this is the same sort of thing, except that the dart is exceeding small, about half the size of a common straight-pin. It's surprisingly easy to hit a hummingbird with the tiny dart. The difficult part is slapping him gently on the cheeks to bring him around after the weighing. That takes a delicate touch indeed." I hadn't actually heard that on the CBC, but it sounded like something you might hear on the CBC, which is almost as good.

What I really did hear on the CBC — weeks later, and from a completely different expert — was that hummingbirds can actually tell colors apart and seem to prefer red flowers. So if you want to try this yourself, all you have to do is paint a flower red, lure a hummingbird, put him to sleep with a stun-pin, weigh him, slap him gently on the cheeks to revive him, and send him back out into the wild.

The CBC interviews people on so many subjects that I wouldn't be at all surprised to turn on the radio one day before I return to the United States and hear somebody being interviewed about Planck's constant, or about the fact that the first two books on the American best-seller list are books about how dumb Americans are. I suspect he'll say that the only evidence those books present for Americans' being dumb is that so many of them will put out good money to buy a book telling them how dumb they are. Then, I would hope, the conversation will turn to hummingbirds.

If I've Told You Once

August 31, 1987

O.K., I HAD TO BE AWAY for a few months. I leave you people in charge. And what do I find when I get back? A mess! An absolute mess!

In the first place, if I've told you once, I've told you a thousand times: you are to keep out of the Middle East. Just tend to your own business. There's no rule that you have to send an aircraft carrier to every single war. The last time I turned my back, it was Lebanon. Now it's the Persian Gulf. Will there ever be a time when I'm able to leave this country with some peace of mind? I wonder.

And there's talk of Gary Hart coming back. Before I went away, I left explicit instructions: nobody is to come back. Now Marcos is talking about coming back. Pretty soon Spiro Agnew is going to want to come back. Yes, I know that Gary Hart didn't steal anything. I'm sure he said it isn't fair to compare him with Spiro Agnew and Baby Doc Duvalier and all those other people I specifically mentioned when I said that nobody is to come back. Fine. But I didn't say that if someone who didn't steal anything wants to come back it's O.K. I said that nobody is to come back. I don't know how many times I have to tell you these things. I really don't.

Now I suppose George Romney's going to want to come back. He didn't steal anything either. Jerry Brown will be back. As it happens — you think you're so smart about letting people come back if they give you some song and dance about not having stolen anything — the people who didn't steal anything are even more trouble when they come back than the people who did. You have to go through the whole process of getting rid of them again, and it can take years. Do you really want to go through that business about Gary Hart's real name and Gary Hart's real age all over again? Do you? I didn't think so.

Which reminds me: What's all this business about candidates having to prove how sensitive they are by whining about the tough life their granny led on the prairie when there was no such thing as fabric softener? What's this about confessing that they used to take all the chocolate Neccos before offering the package to their little brother? I just can't understand this. I leave you people with a bunch of regular politicians trying to stake out their little positions on Guatemala and welfare reform, and I come back to find this gang of kvetches in Iowa weeping all over the corn crop. What did I tell you before I left? I said this plainly: no whining. I'm absolutely certain I told you that before I left. Also, it's on the note taped on the refrigerator door. Will anything ever get done right around here when I'm gone?

And I come back to find the newsstands full of one-shot magazines on the Life of Oliver North, pushing the Elvis one-shots and the Hulk Hogan one-shots back behind the home-repair guides. That's just great. What did I tell you before I left? I said that there would be a lot of talk in the hearings about how real patriots had to protect The Plan from those blabbermouths in Congress, even if it meant skirting the law a tiny bit. Real patriots might even have to lie and cheat and steal — but it was all to protect The Plan. I said to keep one thing in mind during all that talk: it was a stupid plan. Selling arms to those creeps was a stupid plan to begin with. So if Colonel North had actually informed the blabbermouths on the Senate Intelligence Committee about the splendid opportunity he'd been offered in the bazaar, some senator from Tennessee or Georgia would have said, "Son, I don't claim to know a whole lot about the Middle East, but I do know that that's the dumbest plan I've heard since my Uncle Earl tried to train a hog to tap-dance." And that would have been the end of it. I told you that, maybe a hundred times. Why don't you people ever listen?

So now I'm back with a big mess on my hands. Again. This always seems to happen, no matter how many times I've told you that I don't want to find a mess when I get home. And if I've told you once, I've told you a thousand times.

Stalking the Wild Moderate

October 13, 1987

IN THE REAGAN ADMINISTRATION, the first requirement for working in the White House is that you have to be able to recognize a moderate when you see one. You may need to sell him arms. You may need to keep him off the Supreme Court. Either way, you're going to have to know who he is.

Moderates are not that easy to spot. They don't wear capes with the letter *M* sewn on them. They don't wear extreme clothing of any kind. That's the whole point: they're moderate.

When the White House people started talking earlier this year about having tried to make contact with moderate elements in the Iranian government, I found it hard to imagine exactly how they would have gone about it. It's sort of like saying you'd like to make contact with the courteous element in the defensive line of the Chicago Bears. Every time I tried to envision it, the picture that came to my mind was of an outlaw motorcycle gang in the midst of trashing a roadhouse. Tables are being flung through the window. Patrons are being hammered on with beer mugs. Then a man from the local district attorney's office — a tidy-looking man in a three-piece suit and wire-rim glasses — stands up on a table and says, "If I may have your attention for a moment, ladies and gentlemen, I'd very much like to make contact with the moderate elements here."

A man staggers out of the crowd. He's bleeding from a cut on his head. He's holding a chair leg. He looks dazed, but he's obviously trying to make an impression. He's been wanting a submachine gun to impress the other fellows, and he figures that anyone dumb enough to walk into a roadhouse being trashed by a motorcycle gang may be dumb enough to front for him at the local gun dealer's. He places the chair leg carefully on an overturned pinball machine. He rolls down one of his sleeves to hide a tattoo that shows a pit bull terrier tearing apart a bunny rabbit. "Moderate?" he says. "Did someone say something about a moderate? I'm a moderate."

The tidy man from the district attorney's office points a finger at him and says sternly, "You are not the sort of person we want on the Supreme Court."

That couldn't be the way it works. As grateful as I am that this outlaw biker is not going to be a Supreme Court justice, I can't believe that the Administration really goes about its business that way. Maybe if you've been in the White House a long time you learn that moderation is absolutely necessary in some places but not in others, in the way that a free press is absolutely necessary in Nicaragua but not in Chile.

But the pictures that keep coming into my mind make it sound so complicated. Let's say a couple of the Administration's shrewdest operatives were looking for a moderate to sell arms to. They find someone — his code name is Maxie — who seems pretty moderate. At the cocktail lounge where the first meeting takes place, there's some extreme dress — one man at the bar who's outfitted in a flour-sack shirt and cut-off jeans is talking to a man who's wearing a full-dress black velvet jumpsuit — but Maxie's wearing a corduroy sport coat and a knit tie and comfortable-looking crepe-soled shoes. When drinks are ordered, he says he doesn't want any hard liquor but he doesn't want just juice or club soda either. The waiter looks impatient. After a while Maxie settles for a glass of white wine. The men from the White House exchange knowing glances: that was a moderate choice. "Say," one of them says about halfway through drinks, "you wouldn't like to buy any missile launchers, would you? It happens that we've got a special on till the end of the week."

Maxie goes for the deal and also snaps up some anti-tank guns that our guys had thought they might have to get rid of in the Bonanza Days Sidewalk Sale. Then, when everyone has another round in celebration, he orders a triple Wild Turkey on the rocks. Complaining of the heat, he loosens his tie and unbuttons the top buttons of his shirt, revealing a T-shirt that says THE KAISER LIVES. Finally he comes right out with it: he is, in fact, not a moderate but an extremist.

"I'm terribly sorry," one of the men from the Administration says. "In that case we can't sell arms to you."

Maxie looks terribly disappointed. "Don't worry," one of the Administration men says in a soothing voice. "Now that we know you're not a moderate, maybe we can put you on the Supreme Court."

Famous Places

October 19, 1987

AT OUR CORNER BAR the other day, I met a young man who seemed discouraged because nobody in New York appreciated the importance of the town he comes from. I was sympathetic. I know the feeling.

"When I tell people here where I'm from, they act as if it's some little hick town where people gather on Saturday afternoons to watch haircuts," he said. "I don't like to brag, but my hometown happens to be the second-biggest city in Illinois."

"Peoria," the bartender said.

"What?" I said, thinking the bartender was offering some new kind of exotic drink.

"The second-biggest city in Illinois is Peoria," the bartender said.

But the young man, who had understood precisely what the bartender meant, was already shaking his head. "It's not Peoria," he said. "Why does everybody think it's Peoria? Geez! See what I mean?"

As it happened, I knew just where the young man was from. I don't mean that I knew, as the saying goes these days, where he was coming from. I knew that too. But I knew where he was from. Geography's my long suit. My hometown, Kansas City, is famous for its geography teaching, among other things.

Also, I had witnessed this sort of frustration before. Years ago I had a friend in New York who was from Sioux Falls, South Dakota. Before he left home, he assumed that Sioux Falls was universally famous as being the biggest city in five states. He discovered that people in New York tended to think he was from Iowa.

"That's Sioux City you're thinking of," he'd always say. "How can you not even know about a city that's bigger than the biggest city in four other states, not to speak of South Dakota?"

"Is it bigger than Sioux City, then?" the New York people would say.

"None of your business," he'd say. "Let's just skip it."

"I'm sure a lot of people in New York know that your hometown's the second-biggest city in Illinois," I told the young man at the bar. "They just don't like to show off by saying so. Most of them are pretty shy."

"Springfield," the bartender said. "I got ten bucks says it's Springfield." He placed a ten-dollar bill right on the bar in front of the young man from Illinois.

"Save your money for a geography tutor," the young man said, pushing the money back across the bar. "It's not Springfield. Springfield is the third-biggest city in Massachusetts. Otherwise, Springfields don't run to size. Everybody knows that."

As the bartender retreated, I said, "Listen, I know just how you feel. I knew someone in New York from Georgia once."

The young man nodded somberly. "Biggest state east of the Mississippi in area," he said.

"Then you know," I said.

"Yes, I know," he said.

"Well, nobody else around here did," I told him. "And believe me, this guy was desperate for people to know that he came from someplace important, because people would say to him, 'Does everybody where you're from talk funny?' He'd say, 'What do you think is the biggest state east of the Mississippi?' and they'd say, 'Probably Pennsylvania or some hick state like that.' He got so desperate he'd remind everyone he met that Atlanta is the second-highest major city in the United States, even though he was from Milledgeville himself."

The bartender slid by and said in a tone of studied casualness, "I don't suppose it could be Kankakee, could it?" The young man just shook his head. The bartender said, "I didn't really think so," and slid farther down the bar to serve a couple of drafts.

"I guess your Georgia friend finally moved back home," the young man said.

"Well, yes, he did," I said. "But things don't have to be like that." I told the young man about the group sessions we've held on just this subject in an organization of outlanders in New York we call the Association of Displaced Rubes. I invited him to our next meeting. He didn't seem interested, even after I told him that we'd be serving meatloaf and green Jell-O mold.

"Waukegan!" the bartender shouted triumphantly from halfway down the bar. "Jack Benny's hometown!"

The young man looked as if he might cry.

"He's from Rockford, dummy," I said to the bartender. "The second-largest city in the entire state of Illinois."

"Thanks," the young man said. "That helped. I wasn't sure you really knew."

"Kansas City, where I come from, is famous for its geography teaching," I said. "Among other things."

"Maybe I'll come to one of your meetings after all," he said. "I've been missing meatloaf."

Down the bar the bartender was shaking his head in amazement. "Rockford," he said. "Where the hell is Rockford?"

A Noisy Pulpit

October 26, 1987

NOW THAT PRESIDENT REAGAN has held this year's press conference, he'll presumably go back to his custom of shouting occasional answers to some of the questions shouted at him as he boards his helicopter — a form of communication known as prop-glop.

Some people consider prop-glop an undignified way for the President to address the citizenry. I've even heard it suggested that if prop-glop remains President Reagan's principal means of address, the statues of him that may be in American parks someday will show a man ducking under a rotary blade with one hand cupped to his ear and the other hand holding a dog leash. The reporters who have to shout questions toward the helicopter pad have difficulty maintaining their own dignity — I can assure you that under ordinary circumstances reporters are dignified almost to a fault — and in all the excitement they have missed the real story: the helicopter doesn't actually go anywhere.

That's right. It isn't that President Reagan is in a position to be quoted because he happens to be on his way into his helicopter; he's on his way into the helicopter because it has been decided that he should be in a position to be quoted. Some White House flunky may mumble something about Camp David, but once Reagan has given the reply he wanted to give, the pilot just circles around for a while, checks the traffic on the major arteries, and goes back to the White House.

There's more. I happen to know that one person on the helicopter is on board solely to rev the engine whenever there's a question the President doesn't want to hear. That's right. This guy — his name is Rudyard — wears a uniform that makes him look like a copilot, but he's actually an employee of the White House press office. He knows the subjects the President likes to talk about (baseball, old days in Hollywood, the woman who picks up her welfare check in a Cadillac) and the subjects the President doesn't like to talk about (everything else).

Rudyard knows which White House correspondents are apt to ask hostile questions or questions that require answers full of words with two or more syllables in them. Notice that every time Sam Donaldson opens his mouth the engine of President Reagan's helicopter just happens to make a noise that shakes the entire West Wing.

Having Rudyard's skill to depend on was one of the reasons the President's keepers decided a couple of years ago that his views would be disseminated almost entirely through prop-glop. The formal news conference is still available, of course, when the President wants to explain his policies in depth — such as the recent press conference during which, in answer to a question about what had caused the latest unpleasantness on Wall Street, he triumphantly revealed the fact that John Maynard Keynes, whose economic theories have been favored by liberals for many years, "didn't even have a degree in economics."

I'm not certain precisely what effect the President meant that revelation to have, but I am one citizen who found it unsettling. I happen to know that Sir Isaac Newton had his degree in mathematics rather than physics, and I now have the uneasy expectation that the next apple I see fall from a tree might fall straight up. I suspect a lot of people responded the same way, and I can't believe that having thousands of citizens peering nervously at apple trees is the sort of thing that builds confidence in the economy — which is probably why the President's keepers considered the Keynes remark an excellent argument for a return to the helicopter pad.

I see the White House returning to the familiar prop-glop routine. Keepers go over the standard list of quick shouts to see which one might be appropriate for the day's events. The President spends the morning rehearsing "Over my dead body" and "That's news to me" and, just in case he's asked what his reply would be to the latest threat from the Ayatollah, "So's your old lady."

As the President walks under the rotary blade, holding his dog on a leash, the reporters start shouting questions. One of them asks, "Is it true that Orville and Wilbur Wright didn't have any degrees except in animal husbandry?" But Rudyard flicks a switch and the question is lost in the roar of the engine.

"What about the reports that your own economic adviser got his degree in advanced molecular voodoo, Mr. President?" someone else shouts — but in vain, as Rudyard again guns the engine.

"I understand that you're going to have another press conference next year," a voice shouts, quite clearly.

The President stops, and cups his hands to shout. "That's news to me," he says, and then he ducks into the helicopter.

The Medal Gap

December 21, 1987

THE RUSSIANS are ahead of us in medals. I hate to bring this up in the face of all the enthusiasm over the treaty on intermediate nuclear missiles, but the American people deserve to know: there's a medal gap.

Haven't you noticed those Russian generals staring out from the reviewing stand during the May Day parade in Moscow? They've got medals down to their belt buckles. They've got medals so high on their overcoats that if they all suddenly turned their heads to the left, half of them would poke their eyes out on the Siberian Cold Conduct Ribbon. That may be why they always assume everyone's afraid of them — because they wear so many medals.

Every time I see a television clip of generals on the May Day reviewing stand, I expect at least one of them to topple over on his face from the weight of his medals. It's possible that the officer in charge of the reviewing stand has the generals inserted into slots to prevent that. (Notice that they never move.) Or maybe those big, stiff overcoats they wear are tethered to the platform. When it comes to figuring out how to keep people with a lot of medals upright, the Russians must be way ahead of us.

What always used to astonish me about the generals I saw regularly on the May Day reviewing stand was that they wore more medals every year, even though the Russians weren't fighting anybody. Then I realized that the Red Army must award medals for standing on a reviewing stand in the cold looking grim. You get an extra medal if you don't move at all during the parade. If you manage to look as if you couldn't move even if you wanted to, you get a medal for that. Anyone who looks not just grim but positively poisonous gets an oak-leaf cluster. There's a special medal awarded to anyone who doesn't allow the cold to make his nose run; it's called the Stiff Upper Lip Medal.

Our guys just don't have that many medals. By Russian standards, Oliver North testifying before the Iran-Contra Committee looked virtually unadorned — and he strikes me as the sort of military man who wouldn't think of walking into a congressional hearing room unless he was wearing every single one of his medals, even the one he got for flossing after every meal. At some truly bemedaled event in Moscow — the seventieth anniversary of the revolution, for instance, or even an off-year May Day parade — an officer who didn't wear any more medals than North does might not look like a military man at all. They'd take him for a bellhop, maybe, or a train conductor.

For a long time I thought I was the only one who was aware of the medal gap. Then, a couple of weeks ago, I saw an Associated Press item reporting that the United States Army awarded 253,287 medals last year. (The Navy awarded only 22,072.) An Army spokesman told the AP that the Army, going on the theory that a person should get a medal for "doing his job well," had handed out 155,952 Achievement Medals for that alone. Those of you who have never been in the service can believe that 155,952 people in the Army are doing their jobs well if you want to — even if your entire life experience tells you that only about two hundred people in the entire country are truly doing their jobs well, and about a third of those are bartenders.

I prefer to believe that the Army spokesman was being misleading for reasons of security. I believe that the Army is secretly trying to close the medal gap all by itself. I'm rooting for the Army on this one. I think I might find those stone faces on the Moscow reviewing stand less scary if I knew that we had guys with just as many medals. I think I might feel better about my own military career if I had come out with more than the Good Conduct Medal — and if the lieutenant who handed it to me hadn't written "Barely" on it with a ball-point pen.

I see a spiraling medals race. We start awarding a medal every time a soldier stays awake through a Troop Information and Education lecture. The Russians counter with a medal for anyone who gets his boots on the correct feet. ("With our boots, it's sometimes hard to tell," they say to American negotiators in Geneva who have accused them of producing medals beyond any strategic need.) Sooner or later, the weight of the medals outstrips even the Soviet technology for keeping people with medals upright. Both Russian generals and American generals start to topple over on their faces. The world is a safer place.

Considering Designer Garbage Bags

January 11, 1988

"I DON'T THINK I'm going to comment on the invention of the designer garbage bag," I told my wife. "Even I have my limits."

"Do you?" she said.

"O.K., so maybe I don't," I said. It's true that there was a time when I thought I was above commenting on the news that Secretary of State George Shultz may have a tattoo of a tiger on his backside. That time passed.

"When we were at the Marshalls' the other night, Ralph Becker asked me why you never write about who's going to win the Iowa caucuses, the way other columnists do," my wife said.

"Ralph Becker is just the sort of person who would use designer garbage bags," I said.

"I can feel it coming," my wife said.

"In fact, the more I think about it," I continued, "Ralph

Becker, particularly in that weird get-up he had on at the Marshalls', could be described as a designer garbage bag himself."

"Here we go," my wife said. "I knew you couldn't pass up designer garbage bags."

I had already explained to my wife why I never write about who's going to win the Iowa caucuses. It has to do with a little secret — a secret presumably unknown to Ralph Becker as he blithely trots out to the end of his driveway, carrying his coffee grounds and cantaloupe rinds in a mauve and burgundy garbage bag with understated herringbone stripes. The little secret about the millions of words written on who is going to win the Iowa caucuses is this: on the morning after the caucuses, we're all going to know anyway.

That's right. Simple, isn't it? You'd think that after so many primaries all of those other columnists would have figured it out. But I seem to be the only one in the trade who realizes that those interested in the results of any election can skip all the learned analyses of all the sophisticated polls. All they have to do is read the morning newspaper on the day after the balloting; the results are right there every time.

And what will the political pundits do on the morning after the Iowa caucuses? They'll use the results to predict who will win in New Hampshire. Naturally, a lot of them will be wrong. On the day after the 1980 Iowa caucuses, I heard NBC's chief political correspondent say that the showing of George Bush had effectively eliminated Ronald Reagan from the race. In contrast, here's how I called that election on the day after the final balloting in November: Ronald Reagan won.

Of course, I didn't bother to write a column about that. Everybody already knew. What I wrote that week was a column revealing the fact that when Nancy Reagan attended Girls Latin High School in Chicago she was known as Bubbles. Where were the other guys on that one?

"Ralph wonders why you don't ever write about the long-term effect the balance-of-trade figures are going to have on the economy," my wife said.

"I'll bet he does," I said. "I mean, what else does he have to wonder about, except for whether the dominance of purple in the garbage bag he's about to take out is going to make it clash with the red and orange bag that the sanitation men still haven't picked up from yesterday?"

As it happens, the reason I don't write about what long-term effect the balance-of-trade figures are going to have on the economy is simple: I don't have the foggiest idea. That's right. It's another secret of columnizing that the serious columnists haven't caught on to: if you don't have the foggiest idea about something, there's no law requiring you to write about it.

Simple, isn't it? You'd think that most columnists would have caught on by now, but they haven't. If it's the week that everyone's talking about balance of trade, they talk about balance of trade, even if their knowledge of economics is, like mine, limited to whatever can be learned from calculating whether you could live on the interest if you won third prize in the Publishers Clearing House Sweepstakes.

Because I avoid those subjects, I told my wife, I have to find other subjects to write about. Like the invention of the designer garbage bag.

"But what about foreign affairs?" she said.

"I think the Shultz tattoo column pretty much said it all on that subject," I said.

"I don't even know what you mean by 'the invention of the designer garbage bag,' " my wife said.

"A woman in Florida is marketing garbage bags with designs on them," I said. "I read it in the paper."

"You're going to write a column on that!" she said.

"No, I guess not," I finally said. "Even I have my limits."

First-Name Basis

January 18, 1988

THE NEWS THAT President Reagan and Japanese Prime Minister Takeshita were "on a Ron and Noboru basis" might have struck me as more encouraging if I hadn't just hung up on a total stranger who began a phone pitch for Shearson Lehman's financial services by saying, "Hi, Calvin. How are you today?" It would have been a mistake to interpret the fact that the Shearson Lehman man had called me by my first name as an indication of a productive relationship, particularly considering what I called him.

Also, I was aware that the President and Takeshita's predecessor, Yasuhiro Nakasone, were on a Ron and Yasu basis right through the time Japan was gobbling up our international markets, dumping television sets on our docks, shutting out our agricultural products, and underselling us on souvenirs for our own bicentennial celebration.

I suppose the White House might argue that things could have been a lot worse if Nakasone hadn't tried to go easy on somebody he knew well enough to call Ron. It may be, after all, that Reagan said something like, "I'd sure appreciate it if you fellows didn't buy California out from under us while I'm in office, Yasu," and Nakasone said, "No problem, Ron. Anything for a pal."

A couple of commentators pointed out that Reagan might have decided to call the Prime Minister Noboru after mangling the pronunciation of Takeshita so badly in the welcoming ceremony. (The Japanese pronounce Takeshita in about a syllable and a half, presumably because pronouncing it the way it looks makes it sound like a vegetable dish that comes with your choice of miso soup or salad.)

According to that theory, we would have had pretty frigid relations with India in the fifties if Reagan had been President, since he would have called the Indian leader Prime Minister Nehru even in the White House swimming pool rather than risk saying, "It's really good to have you here, Jawaharlal." Foreign-policy analysts might have later concluded that our foreign-policy objectives had shifted toward Africa, since an American President who had been so stiff with a world-renowned Indian seemed absolutely palsy-walsy with the leader of tiny Madagascar — a gentleman Reagan might have called Justin in order to avoid calling him Prime Minister Rakotoniaina.

Also, if our diplomatic strategy is constrained by the limitations of the President's ability to pronounce foreign names, wouldn't our interests in the South Pacific suffer severely if the King of Tonga, on an official White House visit, suddenly said to Reagan, "Just call me Taufa'ahau Tupou IV"?

Could that be how it's done among heads of state — somebody simply breaks the ice by blurting out, "Just call me

Taufa'ahau Tupou IV"? What if the King is known to his friends as Buzzy? How did Reagan know that Prime Minister Nakasone should be called Yasu rather than Yasuhiro, which is what a Shearson Lehman salesman who phoned him at dinnertime in Tokyo to discuss IRA opportunities would have called him?

It would be fairly simple to find out how phone-to-phone peddlers decide to use first names. You could just telephone the chief executive officer of Shearson Lehman around dinnertime — according to the Standard & Poors directory, he's a man named Peter Cohen — and say, "Listen, Peter, I was wondering if you fellows drill in that first-name approach in your Executive Pest Training Program, or is that the sort of thing they teach at Harvard Business School?"

I mention Harvard Business School because there is a theory that our international economic problems can be traced to Harvard Business School's policy of concentrating on the teaching of Money Fiddling 101 while equivalent Japanese institutions teach what is shunned by all ambitious MBAs in this country: the dreary and unfashionable business of manufacturing goods people might want to buy. If the folks at Harvard really are the ones who got us into this mess, maybe they're dumb enough to ignore one of my Uncle Harry's basic rules of life: if someone you don't know starts calling you by your first name, keep your hand on your wallet.

But all of that doesn't tell us anything about how world leaders decide to use first names, or even how they know which first names to use. Is the fact that Yasuhiro Nakasone is known as Yasu the sort of thing the CIA finds out? If our side knows that Mikhail Gorbachev's closest friends still call him by an old law school nickname — Motormouth — is that what President Reagan should call him? Did it take protracted negotiations between lower-level diplomats to get Reagan and Takeshita on a first-name basis, or did Takeshita, on their first meeting, simply say, "Hi, Ronald. How are you today?" Did President Reagan keep his hand on his wallet?

Humble Roots

January 25, 1988

"IT DOESN'T SEEM TO ME that Robert Dole had such a rough childhood back there in Russell, Kansas."

"Daddy, I hope you're not going to start again about how you had to walk ten miles in the snow barefoot just to get to school when you were a boy. I'm kind of late today, and I have a history test."

"When I was a boy, I had to walk ten miles in the snow barefoot just to get to school."

"Maybe this morning I could have the other cereal, Daddy — not the one that has a lifetime supply of riboflavin in each bowl. I think it may be the riboflavin that makes it taste so gross."

"When the river was frozen over, of course, we could cut across it and save a mile or two, assuming we didn't fall through the ice. And we could also take the short cut through the woods. But considering the wolves . . ."

"Daddy, do you think that while you talk you could pour the cereal that you're holding in your hand? I don't want to be late."

"As I walked along, listening for the baying, I used to think: I'm going to work hard, and maybe someday my daughter will have nothing to worry about except which sort of cereal to have for breakfast."

"Well, it didn't work, because I'm also worried about being late to my history test. Also, Aunt Sukey says you only lived five blocks from school."

"That must have been George Bush Aunt Sukey was talking about. George Bush only lived five blocks from school, and that's why the Dole people are saying that he hasn't suffered enough to be President. If you lived five blocks from school, you can be Vice President. But for President, it's a one-mile minimum."

"No, Daddy, George Bush went to boarding school, so he didn't live any blocks from school at all. Could you just pour the cereal? I'll eat the riboflavin kind if you want."

"We didn't have any riboflavin when I was a boy, of course. A word that size would have been way beyond our means. Gruel was what kids had for breakfast where we lived. Leftover gruel. The mothers used to buy it leftover, already kind of prestuck to the bowl."

"Aunt Sukey says Grandma cooked you any kind of eggs you wanted every morning."

"Aunt Sukey doesn't remember things as well as she once did. Some part of her brain probably just froze on one of those bitter-cold mornings when we had to do the farm chores before starting to school, and now that part has finally thawed out and left a puddle that's soaked her long-term memory."

"Aunt Sukey says you never lived on a farm. She says you lived in a regular house on a street in Kansas City."

"Robert Dole must not have a sister or he couldn't make those stump speeches about how he had to work as a soda jerk when he was a boy. She'd be correcting him from the back row: 'But you got all the chocolate ice cream you could eat, Bob. But all the girls came down to the soda fountain to see you, Bob. But whenever it rained or snowed — which it practically never does in Russell, because of the Gulf Stream — Mom drove you to work, Bob.' "

"Aunt Sukey says that Grandma used to drive you the five blocks if there was the tiniest bit of rain. I don't know why you're always talking about the hardships you went through."

"I'm an American father, and it's my role to remind you daily how far I had to come to be in a position to spoil you rotten."

"I don't think making me late for school is spoiling me rotten."

"If that's a hint that I should drive you to school, forget it. All I have to do is drive you to school and some political hatchet man will use it against you in a presidential campaign someday."

"Aunt Sukey says you had a perfectly comfortable childhood."

"Who is this Aunt Sukey you keep talking about, anyway?"

"She's your sister, Daddy — the person who grew up with you, five blocks from school."

"Sister? I don't remember any sister. I remember walking through that blizzard alone. I remember being out on that ice alone. I remember going through those woods alone. A guy like Bob Dole wouldn't understand what it's like growing up without a sister."

"I thought you said that Bob Dole must not have a sister."

"Things were rough, I can tell you."

"Things are still rough, Daddy. This childhood's so hard I can't even seem to get any breakfast."

"Here, have some cereal."

"No thanks, Daddy. I'm afraid I'll be late. I'm going to have to cut through the woods as it is."

Theories I Have Known

February 1, 1988

FINALLY THERE'S SOMETHING in the news to dampen Jimmy the Greek's concern that every single aspect of American athletics is going to be taken over by blacks who have been bred to have long thighs: in a story about a black FBI man who was tormented by his colleagues, one of the agents involved said to investigators in passing, "The reason blacks can't swim as well as whites is because their bone density is thicker." Presumably this means that members of the Olympic swim team can stop worrying about black competition. Whether it means that the rest of us can stop worrying about the FBI is something else again.

I should acknowledge right away that I myself spent the first year of the Second World War believing that the Japanese had yellow blood. When I was a child, in fact, I picked up all sorts of misinformation about Asian anatomy — some of it I'd just as soon not mention here, even now that we're being absolutely honest with each other — and I was also privy to some pretty startling theories about black people. I use the phrase "privy to" not just because it sounds fancy but because out behind the privy at Camp Osceola, the Kansas City–area Boy Scout camp, was where I heard a lot of these things.

I was told, for instance, that black people had thicker skulls than white people, making it easier for them to hoe cotton all day in the sun and less dangerous for them if they were hit by a pitched ball. I was told again and again that if you had tiny half-moons on your fingernails — or maybe if you didn't have tiny half-moons on your fingernails; I've forgotten which — you had "black blood in you." The phrase was not meant literally. I want it on the record that by the time I was at Camp Osceola I knew that all blood was red.

When I was a reporter in the South in the early sixties, some white people who were trying to explain why it wouldn't be a good idea to allow black people to vote let me in on theories that even the savants at Camp Osceola hadn't known. Any number of times, for instance, I was told that black people could understand specific instructions but couldn't deal with anything abstract. As it happens, I've always had trouble grasping anything abstract myself — even something no more abstract than that theory. "What do you mean?" I said to the first person who told it to me. "Give me an example."

"An example?" he said.

"Yeah, an example," I said. "Something specific."

By that time, of course, I was old enough to dismiss all such yard-sale anthropology as what I'd come to think of as "yellow-blood stuff." Now, years later, we're told that there are FBI agents who still believe the race theories they heard out behind the privy at Boy Scout camp, not to speak of FBI field-office directors who think that agents who do things like deface the family pictures of one of their fellow agents are having some good clean fun. I can imagine one of the Osceola theorists explaining that one: "Black people don't mind having their families insulted because they're lacking this whatzis we've got in a certain part of the brain."

All this was revealed the same week we found out that the FBI spent four years collecting information on people like nuns and trade unionists who oppose the Administration's policies in Central America. I find myself still looking for some specifics that my nonabstract mind can grasp. What, specifically, justified four years of spying on people who were breaking no laws? What, specifically, is so much fun about insulting someone's children? These days, citizens can ask such specific questions about the FBI without fear, we're assured, because the agency has been reformed. Unless it hasn't. In that case, maybe I can expect an FBI agent to come around some night to inspect my fingernails.

Who They Are

February 15, 1988

PAT ROBERTSON is not a television evangelist. I heard him say so. He's a successful broadcasting executive. If the Pope were running in the presidential primaries, he would be the chief executive officer of a giant multinational outfit with headquarters in Rome. Jimmy Bakker is a retired broadcasting figure and business leader. Jessica Hahn is a model. Let's keep everything straight.

George Bush is a Texas wildcatter who built a business the hard way. He lived ten years in a town where if you asked for hors d'oeuvres at the country club they brought you Fritos. We're talking here about the hard way. So don't go calling him a preppie who had everything handed to him on a silver platter — not unless you're looking for a mouthful of Chiclets. This guy is tough.

And don't go calling Tammy Bakker what you were calling her that got such a big laugh at Kiwanis the other day (I don't even want to repeat it). Tammy Bakker is a former broadcasting figure and a composer of popular songs. The leaders of the *contras* are the moral equivalent of our Founding Fathers. Donna Rice is also a model. Got it?

Gary Hart is a populist. Richard Gephardt is a populist. Robert Dole is a populist. Paul Simon is a populist. Jack Kemp is a populist. George Bush is a tough populist. Pierre Du Pont is a populist. Prince Philip, the Duke of Edinburgh, is a populist, although, as they say in Iowa, not so's you'd know it. Henri d'Orleans, Count of Paris and Pretender to the Throne of France, is a populist. So are they all — all populists.

Robert Dole is a poor boy from Russell, Kansas. So don't go calling him a sophisticated Senate insider — not unless you're prepared to hear a lot of poormouthing about what it was like back then. Bob Dole built a rough childhood the hard way. Here's what was hard about it: he didn't realize he'd ever be able to use it in a presidential campaign. He thought it was nothing but a rough childhood. Dole must have figured that when he grew up he was going to make a living the way other people in Russell, Kansas, did — as a hardware store proprietor or an oil-well capper or a seed salesman. A rough childhood wouldn't have done a hardware store proprietor much good.

Imagine the proprietor of a hardware store pulling a customer aside and saying, "I had it rough back then, I can tell you that."

"Well, I guess a lot of us around here had it sort of rough, Bob," the customer would say. "I'm kind of in a hurry for that number four sprocket, Bob, if you could just maybe take a look for it."

Maybe somebody in Russell — somebody like that nice Miss Hester, at the library — realized that a rough childhood would stand Bob Dole in good stead someday. "You ought to be grateful that you're shoveling grain in this ninety-five-degree heat,

Robert," she'd say. "Because in a presidential campaign someday that sort of thing may allow you to make a tough Texas wildcatter look like a spoiled rich kid."

"Well, since you think it's so nice, Miss Hester," Dole would say, "maybe you'd like to finish shoveling that carload over there."

"If you're going to be President, Robert," Miss Hester would say, "you're going to have to watch that smart tongue of yours."

Anyway, Robert Dole is a poor boy from Russell, Kansas. Edwin Meese is innocent until proven guilty. He's innocent until proven guilty on the Wedtech thing and innocent until proven guilty on the telephone contract thing and innocent until proven guilty on the Iraq pipeline thing and innocent until proven guilty on the Iran-*contra* thing. Edwin Meese is the chief executive officer of a large multi-innocent outfit with headquarters in Washington.

Remember: Pat Robertson is a broadcasting executive who ran the fifth-largest cable network in the country. (The people who run the first four largest cable networks in the country have decided not to run for President this time around.) So don't go calling him a television evangelist — not unless you want to make him mad enough to send a hurricane your way. Broadcasting executives can do that sort of thing. Jessica Hahn is a model. Donna Rice is a model. So are they all — all models. Not George Bush. George Bush is a Texas wildcatter who built a business the hard way.

Third Persons

February 22, 1988

WHEN ROBERT DOLE TALKS about Bob Dole doing this and Michael Dukakis talks about Mike Dukakis doing that, they apparently don't realize that Calvin Trillin is not going to vote for anybody who speaks of himself in the third person. Calvin Trillin is not that sort of guy.

Almost ten years ago Calvin Trillin stated publicly that he would never vote for a candidate who referred to himself in the third person. At the time, Calvin Trillin said that the only public figure of recent memory who was able to get away with that sort of thing was Satchel Paige, the philosopher king of several pitching staffs, and that Ole Satch, as he sometimes called himself, had the grace not to run for public office.

A reader from Missouri wrote to Calvin Trillin to say that Ole Satch had in fact run for office a couple of times in Calvin Trillin's own hometown of Kansas City. So Calvin Trillin was wrong. Calvin Trillin is the sort of guy who admits it when he's wrong, although Calvin Trillin would also like to take this opportunity to remind the reader from Missouri that nobody likes a nit-picker.

Calvin Trillin is going to stop talking in the third person himself now, because, having made his point, he doesn't want to drive his readers absolutely bonkers. (Calvin Trillin is not that sort of guy.) But first he's going to mention one more rule in the same general area: Calvin Trillin also doesn't vote for people who speak in the first person plural. When a candidate says, "We appreciate your support," Calvin Trillin has one question: You and who else?

In fact, Calvin Trillin doesn't even write in the first person plural. We gave it up the first time we found ourselves writing, "We felt we had to blow our nose." As it happens, that's the same phrase that kept us from referring to ourselves as "one," since one didn't really like the sound of the phrase "one felt one had to blow one's nose." Now that Pierre Du Pont is out of the race, there's probably no danger that any of these people are going to refer to themselves as "one," but one wouldn't want to vote for the one who did. One isn't that sort of guy.

There's plenty of danger, though, that they're going to continue to refer to themselves in the third person. Some of them have talked about themselves that way for so long that you'd think they'd be on a first-name basis with themselves. But Dukakis never says, "Mike can do for America what he did for Massachusetts." Given Robert Dole's reputation for geniality and warmth, I suppose we can count ourselves lucky that he doesn't refer to himself in the third person as "the senator."

I don't mean to single out Dole and Dukakis as the principal third persons in this race. I assume that all the candidates talk this way — although from what everybody else says about Richard Gephardt's remaking of his positions for the campaign, I wouldn't be surprised to hear that he occasionally refers to himself in the third person by the wrong name.

What I wonder is why they do it. I'm trying to avoid the simplest explanation: delusions of grandeur. After all, one of these guys is going to be President. What I would like to believe is that the average presidential candidate finds what he says so embarrassing that he gets some comfort from assigning it to some third person — even a third person who happens to be himself. From the last few presidential campaigns, after all, it's hard to escape the feeling that the man who becomes President of the United States these days is someone willing to spend a year or two embarrassing himself for the opportunity to spend four years embarrassing the rest of us.

Just the glimpse I've had of Michael Dukakis's mother during the campaign makes me pretty sure that young Mike would have been ordered from the dinner table for a hint of the silly boasting that all presidential candidates engage in daily. So he assigns the silly boasting to someone named Mike Dukakis. The danger, of course, is that it can get to be a habit with presidential candidates, like automatically waving to the crowd whenever they emerge from an airplane. I hope that former candidates who have been forgotten no longer wave whenever they emerge from an airplane. It could be embarrassing, and their embarrassment is supposed to be over. I hope — we hope, one hopes, Calvin Trillin hopes — that when all of this is over, the senator from Kansas doesn't find himself saying at dinner some evening, "No, Bob Dole doesn't want another baked potato. Bob Dole is not that sort of guy."

Comforting Thoughts

February 29, 1988

FIRST I READ ABOUT a study in Meriden, Connecticut, which indicated that talking to yourself is a perfectly legitimate way of getting comfort during a difficult time. Then I saw an item about research at Yale demonstrating that stress seems to be reduced in some people by exposing them to the aromas of certain desserts. Then I started talking to myself about desserts with aromas I find soothing. Then I felt a lot better. Isn't science grand?

I didn't feel perfect. One thing that was bothering me — this is what I decided after I was asked by myself, "Well, what seems to be the trouble, guy?" — was that the ten most popular methods of comforting yourself listed in the Meriden study didn't mention sniffing desserts, even though Yale, where all the sniffing research was going on, is only about twenty miles down the road. Does this mean that some of these scientists are so busy talking to themselves that they don't talk to each other? It got me so upset that I went to the back door of a bakery in our neighborhood to sniff the aroma of chocolate chip cookies. I was talking to myself the whole time, of course.

"What the Yale people think," I said to myself, "is that a person's soothed by the smell of, say, chocolate chip cookies because it brings back pleasant memories, like the memory of his mother baking chocolate chip cookies."

"What if his mother always burned the chocolate chip cookies?" I replied.

"Are you talking about my mother?"

"Whose mother do you think I'm talking about?" I said. "We're the only one here."

"Were those cookies burnt?"

"What do you think all that black stuff was?"

"I thought that was the chocolate chips."

"No, she always forgot the chocolate chips."

I wasn't finding the conversation very comforting at all. I don't like to hear anyone making light of my mother's chocolate chip cookies, even me. I must have raised my voice, because the next thing I knew, the baker had come out to see what was going on.

Even though the Meriden study had shown that being with someone else was the most comforting thing of all — it finished ahead of listening to music and even watching TV — I saw right away that being with the baker wasn't going to be much more comforting than talking to myself. He said, "What are you, some kind of nut case, or what?"

I told him that I was engaging in two therapies that had been scientifically proven effective: sniffing chocolate chip cookies and talking to myself. He told me that I owed him two dollars and fifty cents. "For sniffing, we charge a buck and a quarter a dozen," he explained.

"How do you know I sniffed two dozen?" I asked.

"We got ways," he said.

I told him that according to the research done at Yale, certain odors caused the brain to produce alpha waves, which are associated with relaxation. I told him that in my case the odor of chocolate chip cookies — particularly slightly burnt chocolate chip cookies — was such an odor. I told him that he ought to be proud to confirm the scientific research done at one of the great universities of the English-speaking world. That alone, I told him, ought to be payment enough for whatever small part of the aroma of his chocolate chip cookies I had used up with my sniffing.

He thought about it for a moment. Then he said, "Take a walk, buddy."

I was happy to. As it happens, going for a walk finished tenth in the Meriden study, just behind recalling pleasant memories. Naturally, I talked to myself on the way.

"Maybe I can find someplace to smell what the Yale people call 'spiced apple,' " I said to myself. "They found that the smell of spiced apple is so effective that with some people it can stop panic attacks."

"But I don't know what spiced apple smells like," I replied. "Spiced with what?"

That was bothering me enough that my walk wasn't actually very soothing. I thought about bolstering it with some of the other activities on the list, but reading or watching TV seemed impractical. Prayer was also on the list, but praying for the aroma of spiced apple seemed frivolous.

I walked faster and faster. It occurred to me that I might be getting a panic attack. Desperately I tried to recall some pleasant memories. I recalled the time before I knew about the Meriden list, when I talked to myself only in private. I recalled the time before I knew about the Yale research and didn't have to worry about finding any spiced apple. Then I felt a lot better. I didn't feel perfect, but you can't always feel perfect.

Try, Try Again

March 14, 1988

JACK KEMP'S PROMISE in his withdrawal speech to try again someday did not strike me as a silver lining. I don't mean that as a reflection on Kemp as a candidate. In fact, I was beginning to find things I liked about Kemp as a candidate, even though he has always struck me as one quarterback who has a defensive tackle's grasp of economics. I almost always find things to like about a candidate around the time he withdraws.

What disturbed me about Kemp's promise to return was that it reflected the increasingly widespread belief that in order to become President you have to run for the office more than once. The two major Republican candidates left in the race after Kemp's withdrawal, George Bush and Robert Dole, have both run for the nomination before — and for all I know, Pat Robertson has himself run a couple of times in never-never land.

It seems to me that when it comes to presidential politics the American people have finally arrived at one, and only one, belief sufficiently widespread to be considered a consensus: the sort of person willing to subject himself to the indignities and absurdities of running for the presidential nomination is not the sort of person we'd want in the job. Now that we all know that, we're told that the person we're most likely to have in the job is the sort of person willing to put up with the indignities and absurdities of running for the presidential nomination at least twice.

The day Kemp withdrew, I saw Robert Dole on the television news bouncing a balloon back and forth with a grade-school child in Illinois. The balloon bouncing was what the campaign people think of as a photo opportunity. The child participating was too young to vote in the Illinois primary, although I suppose there are still precincts in the state where you might have a fair chance of registering him if you know the right people.

Dole had a tight little smile on his face. He didn't look happy. He had already jettisoned half of his campaign staff by then, and Republican leaders were urging him to withdraw before he finished providing the Democrats with all of the nasty, mean-spirited, and disturbingly persuasive lines they could possibly use in running against George Bush in the fall.

I figured that while he was bouncing the balloon he was thinking, "Why am I doing this? Why am I bouncing a balloon for the evening news? I'm a grown-up." And I was thinking, "You're right, senator. You're a person of some substance. This is not for you. Pack it in." Then I realized that Robert Dole's campaign must be about over, because I was beginning to feel some sympathy for him.

Part of my magnanimity at the moment of a presidential candidate's exit, I'll admit, may come from pure relief. When any candidate withdraws, one tiny voice I hear just above my left ear says, "Well, at least we don't have to worry about this guy trying to run the country." I never repeat that, of course. When someone is walking off the field, I can always scratch around and find a few kind words on a back shelf somewhere —

although I'll admit that Hart's second withdrawal found the cupboard almost bare.

Some of my warm feelings might also be traced to the hope, almost always misplaced, that the withdrawing candidate may have actually seen the light: his election is not so essential to the nation's survival that he simply must leave his family and his job for a couple of years of living in motels and trying to remember the first names of county chairmen he finds marginally loathsome.

I had that hope for Walter Mondale in 1976, when he pulled out of the race against Jimmy Carter saying that he didn't have the stomach for it. But back he came. Back they all come. In the view of the cynics, what Mondale had really been saying was that he was running out of campaign funds and didn't have a chance. The cynics are probably right, but I still think of Mondale's departure when I try to recall a gesture in presidential campaigns that seemed, just for a moment, presidential.

Tan-Plan Action

March 28, 1988

S. HAS A WEEK on a sunny island, and she desperately needs to catch some rays. She knows that skin tone peaks at precisely age sixteen and a half, so this is her last chance. Her goal is the streaky-blond look. She has a tan-plan.

She will let nothing stand in the way of the implementation of her tan-plan. Failure would mean losing her last chance. Failure would also mean looking pasty-faced all spring, particularly compared with a girl in her class named T. — who, S. has to admit, would be attractive with the right tan, if you like a sort of cheap look. T. is on another sunny island, with her own tan-plan. S. knows that T.'s tan-plan will be implemented. T. is a determined person. No, S. is determined; T. is pushy.

S. knows that an attempt to block her tan-plan will be made by the Sun Police. The Sun Police have an exceedingly narrow mission. They do nothing but try to keep sixteen-year-old girls out of the sun. They win promotions in direct proportion to the pastiness of the face of the person whose case they're on. S. has always managed to elude them.

A lot of research has gone into S.'s tan-plan. Physicists and mathematicians have done complicated calculations concerning the burning and tanning capacities of the sun at certain angles — the angle of the sun and the angle of the person catching the rays. This and other information has been refined by a boy named N., a slightly wonky but eagerly helpful math whiz in S.'s class, to produce an Effective Exposure Pattern (EEP) that is tailor-made for S. As it happens, N. thinks S. looks fine even when her face is the color of Elmer's glue.

The tan-plan calls for S. to start her week on the sunny island by covering herself with number sixteen sunblock and lying in the sun for precisely seventeen minutes, beginning at ten-fifteen in the morning — unless it's a cloudy day, in which case she lies in the sun for eighteen minutes, beginning at five after eleven.

Unless there's a breeze of more than six miles an hour, in which case she goes back to the seventeen-minute start. This is assuming that the reflecting capacity of the sand tests in the normal range, according to a color chart S. carries with her at all times. This is also assuming that she has plugged herself into her Walkman and is listening to a heavy metal group. N., squirrelly little genius that he is, has factored into the EEP the slight involuntary body movement of someone listening to the heavy metal beat.

Then S. is scheduled to move into the shade. Then the sun. Then the shade. It's all in the tan-plan. In the first four days there are 139 movements in and out of the sun. At the end of the fourth day she'll have reached her preliminary goal: a base. Everything has been worked out. Some people believe that N. may someday win the Nobel Prize for all of this. N. doesn't want the Nobel Prize. He wants S. to smile at him.

The first day on the sunny island is sunny. S. is covered in number sixteen. She is plugged into her Walkman. The angles are correct. The sand has passed its test. At precisely ten-fifteen in the morning, S. puts her tan-plan into effect. Everything is on schedule. Then the Sun Police appear.

Around the department, the person handling S.'s case is known as a tough cop. She has tried, unsuccessfully, to put S. away — out of the sun — before, on other sunny islands and in Florida. She looks a lot like S.'s mother. The tough Sun Cop's partner is a rumpled veteran of many beaches. He has been burnt before.

Sun Cops carry no firearms. They have only one weapon: nagging. Mostly they say, "Will you please get out of the sun this minute!" S. is not worried about the Sun Police. They've got nothing on her. She's got a tan-plan. The Sun Police are worried about S. They don't understand the tan-plan. They've met N., and they think he's lucky to find his way to school. They nag a lot. Usually S. doesn't answer. Sometimes she says, "I'll get out in just a second." After the fourth day she says, "I've got my base."

After a week the Sun Police agree about what they'll have to put in their report: S. has eluded them again. She has managed to implement her tan-plan precisely. She has a streaky-blond look. She looks gorgeous.

No Gossip in Russia

April 11, 1988

IN A RECENT NEWSPAPER STORY there was a quote from Liz Smith, the gossip columnist of the *New York Daily News*, that I couldn't get out of my mind: "Remember, they don't have gossip in Russia."

This was said in the context of trying to get some perspective on a widely publicized feud between two other gossip columnists — in these grim times, Ms. Smith pointed out, being able to devote a lot of attention to something so frivolous could be seen as a luxury — but it had a different effect on me. It made me realize that there are 262 million Russians who don't know the first thing about Elizabeth Taylor.

Once I began thinking about those Russians, I envisioned them in every part of their daily routines. I could see them at the tractor factory, where they're under a lot of pressure because their previous efforts to meet higher production quotas resulted in sending out tractors whose motors tended to fall out at inopportune moments. (There is actually no opportune moment for a tractor's motor to fall out; I'm just trying to be diplomatic.) I could see them at the market, buying beets and cabbage and potatoes — or maybe, now that Gorbachev has begun to restructure the entire society, instant borscht. I could see them settling down after dinner in comfortable armchairs to read *Pravda* or watch the Soviet State Television's weekly prime-time family drama based on the technical operation of a hydroelectric plant in Sredne Kolymsk. All that time, they're wondering about Elizabeth Taylor. "What's with Liz?" they say to one another. "Is she keeping her weight down? Who's she married to these days? What ever happened to Eddie Fisher?"

The questions draw only shrugs. Nobody knows. *Pravda* doesn't have a gossip columnist. It runs editorials now and then saying that gossip is a symptom of bourgeois decadence. Thousands of people secretly listen to the Voice of America on shortwave radio, hoping to hear some news of Elizabeth Taylor, but all they hear is reports of atrocities by Russian troops in Afghanistan.

Some gossip seeps in, of course. Packages sent by Russian immigrants in Brooklyn to their relatives back home in Tbilisi and Kislovodsk contain economy-size bottles of diet root beer wrapped in old copies of New York tabloids. Western tourists who pass through Leningrad may leave behind a copy of *People* magazine that the chambermaid recovers from the wastebasket, painstakingly irons, and then passes around, hidden behind the cover of *Soviet Agricultural Pioneer News*.

What little gossip there is, though, is often old and inaccurate. People who are separating the wheat from the chaff on a collective farm in the Ukraine pass the time by arguing about whether Barbara Hutton is going to leave Ali Khan. Old men in Bashkir think Elizabeth Taylor is still married to Nicky Hilton. When all is said and done, they don't have any gossip in Russia.

When I finally came to grips with that fact, it made me realize that there are a lot of other things they don't have in Russia — TV game shows and miniature golf and takeout Chinese food and drive-in banks and commercials for bran cereals. No wonder they don't seem to understand what we're talking about when we try to negotiate with them. As Lenin himself used to say, they don't know where we're coming from.

All of this made me think that we may be on the wrong track with cultural exchange programs that send the Cleveland Symphony to Russia and the Kirov Ballet here. The Russians are familiar with symphonies. We're familiar with ballets. Maybe it would be better if we were both sent things we'd otherwise know nothing about. I don't know what the Russians could send us — that's the whole point — but we could send them something like gossip.

We'd start with a program to teach them how to have a domestic gossip industry. It would fit right in with glasnost. First, we train a lot of press agents, reminding the Soviet authorities of an old Russian proverb: a gossip columnist without press agents is a dairy farmer without cows. Then the Soviet columnists start doing some local items ("The soulful tête-à-tête between Minsk party heavy Vladimir Selomentsky and Ukrainian harvest committee Deputy First Secretary Tanya Gunestkov at Boris Karputsky's après–May Day Parade bash has tongues wagging all over Zvenigorodka"). Gradually they begin including items about American gossip-column regulars — the usual charity-ball trotters and glitz-hounds and previously owned debutantes. Then Frank Sinatra. Then, precisely on the schedule laid out in the new cultural exchange treaty, Elizabeth Taylor.

Kiss and Tell

April 25, 1988

DURING THE FLAP about Larry Speakes's memories of the Reagan White House, did it occur to you that one of your kids may someday publish a kiss-and-tell book about your administration?

Never gave it a thought? Fine. Maybe you don't have anything to worry about. Maybe it's perfectly O.K. that you lied to your Cousin Irma — the one with the big teeth and the truly irritating laugh — when she phoned to say she was in town from Providence for a couple of days and you said that unfortunately you couldn't see her because your entire neighborhood was under quarantine for emotional asthma. Maybe the fact that your middle son began writing furiously in a notebook as you spoke meant simply that, by coincidence, he had just thought of some interesting calculus proofs and wanted to jot them down so he could discuss them with his pals at the drive-in later that evening. Then again, maybe not.

You've got nothing to hide? Fine. Then don't bother to make an announcement that from now on breakfast is off the record. There may be no significance at all in the fact that your younger daughter — the one who responded to being grounded for six weeks by saying that she'd get even with you someday — has acquired the habit of placing a recording device next to her cereal bowl and flicking it on whenever the conversation turns to tax avoidance. By the time she published anything, the statute of limitations would have run out anyway. I think.

Nobody would be interested in the story of an ordinary family? Maybe not. But remember how interested everyone was in the ordinary family those documentary film makers snooped on for a public television series a few years ago. Maybe your family is actually a little juicier than that family was. Maybe that's precisely the argument one of your kids is making to a literary agent — somebody like Irving (Swifty) Lazar — at this very moment.

You're confident that your kids are too loyal to think of embarrassing you by revealing those insignificant little arguments about money or the scene over the boyfriend with three earrings and a modified Mohawk or the incident involving the Thanksgiving turkey and the cat? Maybe — although, speaking as what my wife has occasionally referred to as "nearly a professional writer," I have to say that the business with the Thanksgiving turkey seems to me almost irresistible. (I see it as a chapter on its own.) I suppose Nancy Reagan was also confident about her daughter's loyalty, just before the novel came out.

You're certain that you're a lot closer to your children than the Reagans are to theirs? Well, we're not talking about a fast track here, but you're probably right. On the other hand, that gives your kids more material. One of the theories about why the Reagans' younger daughter chose to publish her kiss-and-tell book in the form of a novel is that she hadn't spent enough time with her parents to gather any significant amount of factual information. That wouldn't be a problem for your kids. They were there. They saw what happened to the turkey. They knew and loved that cat.

Am I worried about this happening in my own house? No, as a matter of fact, I'm not. Yes, I realize that there are some eerie similarities between our own operation and the Reagan White House. Yes, I realize that someone could probably draw a parallel between what the White House sometimes describes as President Reagan's hands-off management style and what my daughter is trying to express when she turns to me at breakfast and says, "Pops, you're losing it."

Despite that, I'm confident that we won't be seeing any kiss-and-tell books on our administration. For one thing, the story has already been told. It came out years ago as "The Ozzie and Harriet Show." Nobody wants to hear about that kind of thing anymore — shrewd teenagers manipulating the grown-ups, wise Mom managing to work things out without Pop's being embarrassed any more than necessary, Pop in his cardigan telling little jokes in a futile attempt to hide the fact that he hasn't the foggiest idea of what's going on.

You say that sounds very much like the White House, with the guys in the National Security Council basement as the teenagers and Howard Baker as the mom? Then it's a story that is even more dog-eared than I thought. Unlike your story. Your story is fresh. I think it has great paperback potential. I see the Thanksgiving turkey on the jacket, or maybe the cat. You don't think that could ever happen? Maybe not. But maybe.

Just Desserts

May 2, 1988

I DON'T KNOW WHY I continue to read *Business Week*'s annual issue on executive pay. It's bound to be discouraging. This year, for instance, when I learned that two executives of a company called Waste Management made more than thirteen million dollars apiece in 1987, I couldn't help remembering that many years ago my father suggested waste disposal as a field I might think about entering myself. Yet another lost opportunity.

As I remember the conversation in which the subject of careers in waste management came up, my father said something like, "If you don't straighten out, you're going to find yourself working on a garbage truck."

I wish I could report that I countered by predicting the sort of salary a good waste management executive might hope to command a few decades down the road, what with the growing problem of solid waste accumulation in this country. Even if I had, though, I suspect my father would have said that most of the solid waste in this country seemed to be accumulating in my bedroom. It's hard to win one of those arguments, particularly if you've been having a little trouble in first-year algebra.

Oddly enough, I was already familiar with an economic theory that encouraged a career in waste management. It was a theory I'd heard propounded by a world history teacher we called Colonel Jim, a former military man who had white hair and a yellowish mustache and a voice with the kind of slur that most colonels acquire only late in the evening.

According to the word around our high school, Colonel Jim learned the names of only two or three people in each of his classes, and those people were assured of receiving A's no matter how profound their ignorance of the subject. Because of that, the first few days of the term in Colonel Jim's class were packed with entertainment as one student or another tried to imprint himself on the Colonel's mind — reciting the Gettysburg Address in answer to a question about the ancient Greeks, falling to the floor with a groan in the hope of being remembered as "the one with the bellyache," offering to wash the blackboard even though Colonel Jim rarely bothered to write anything on it.

The class in which Colonel Jim revealed his economic theory was almost as entertaining. Basically, the Colonel believed that people should be paid pretty much in direct proportion to the unpleasantness of their job. He said he couldn't understand why someone like a banker, who sat around all day in a comfortable office, should get more money than, say, a garbageman.

"Think of the garbageman on an August day!" the Colonel would say, with considerable feeling. He then launched into a graphic description of a hot and nearly exhausted garbageman wrestling heavy cans of reeking garbage into the truck. The

Colonel, it turned out, had a gift for evocative description that could never have been guessed by those who had heard him slur over the Roman Empire in fifteen or twenty minutes. The part of the garbage saga I remember best was a description of how some of the garbage would invariably escape from the can as it was lifted into the truck and spill down the sleeve of the garbageman's shirt.

"Disgusting!" a student would shout from the back row at that point. "Someone stop him!" another student would shout. "I'm going to be sick!" The "one with the bellyache" would fall from his desk to the floor, clutching at his stomach, and people in nearby seats would begin to shout, "Boy down! There's a boy down in the back row!"

When I read in *Business Week* about the two well-compensated Waste Management executives — one of them, Phillip B. Rooney, made $14,276,000 last year; the other, Donald F. Flynn, went home with $13,217,000 — it naturally occurred to me that someone may be putting Colonel Jim's theory of just rewards into effect. After all, the chairman of Sara Lee, a man surrounded by cakes, made only $5,788,000.

I realize that someone who pulls down thirteen million dollars a year in waste management is in no danger of personally catching a sleeveful of garbage. Still, think of all those hot August days when Mr. and Mrs. Donald F. Flynn emerge from their luxury hotel, climb into a taxi, and hear the driver say, "You folks must be in town for the waste management convention." Think of all the times a charming and elegant woman at a posh dinner party has turned to the man on her left and said, "And what do you do, Mr. Rooney?" I'm not sure Colonel Jim would consider that sort of experience worth thirteen million dollars a year, but in his scheme of things it's definitely worth something.

Like, Really

May 31, 1988

THINGS HAVE FINALLY RETURNED to normal among the teenagers I know, after a spring filled with vocabulary tension brought on by the Scholastic Aptitude Tests. "Relax," I kept saying to S., the teenager I know best, as the pressure in her crowd mounted. "I read that a lot of colleges don't pay much attention to SAT scores anyway. Also, you can always go to work in the dime store."

"Relaxing would be a herculean task — meaning a task very difficult to perform," S. said. "Because among my friends there's no dearth of anxieties. A dearth is like a paucity — a scarcity or scanty supply. In fact, most of the people I know have a plethora of anxieties — a surfeit, an overabundance."

All of S.'s friends were talking that way. One evening, when we were giving S.'s friend D. a ride uptown, D. said, "I'll be on the corner of Thirteenth and Sixth Avenue, in proximity to the mailbox."

"In proximity?" I said.

"Kind of in juxtaposition to the mailbox," D. said. "That's a placing close together or side by side. If I get tired while I'm waiting, you'll find me contiguous to the mailbox."

"What if someone wants to mail a letter?" I asked.

"If that eventuality — that contingent event, that possible occurrence or circumstance — occurs," D. said, "I'll move."

This is not the way teenagers normally speak. Ordinarily they don't need many long words — or, for that matter, many words of any size. Some of them can make do for days on end with hardly any words at all beyond the word "like," as in the sentence "Like, I said, 'Like, what?' and he was like, 'Like, O.K.' "

As it happens, listening to someone who says "like" every second or third word can get irritating. When S.'s father brings that fact to her attention, in an appropriately courteous and dignified manner ("If you say 'like' once more at this dinner table, you're going to be put in a foster home!"), S. can explain why each use of the word is absolutely logical.

She explains that "like" in some cases is used the way a non-teenager would use "more or less" or "sort of." She explains that "he was like" means not exactly "he said" but something more on the order of "his speech and his manner indicated." Her explanations sound persuasive, which her father finds almost as irritating as listening to someone who says "like" every second or third word.

In fact, S. has logical explanations for a lot of teenage talk. She can explain why it's O.K. to use "stupid" or "crazy" as adverbs meaning "very" or "truly," so that you could say either "That guy is stupid crazy" or, if he happens to be stupider than he is crazy, "That guy is crazy stupid." She can explain the difference between snapping and ranking — both words for harassing or insulting — well enough to correct her parents at the dinner table, so that if her father says, "S., stop ranking on

A.," she might say, "That wasn't a rank. It was more of a harsh snap." S. is, like, a scholar of teenspeak.

When I thought about that fact this spring, it occurred to me that the teenagers I know wouldn't have been feeling any tension at all if only the SATs were given in their own language. ("Like is to like as: a) like is to like, or b) like is to like.") The problem emerged from the Educational Testing Service's stubborn insistence on giving the test in English. That hardly seems fair.

Think of how difficult it would be for nonteenagers to bone up on vocabulary if they were required to take a test in teenspeak. I can imagine, say, two golfers of middle years and competitive temperaments ready to hit their drives on the first green. Al swats his drive right down the center of the fairway and says, "Super-fly fresh! That, as you may know, is an exclamation indicating approval or delight."

"The vocabulary test is not for another month," Jack says irritably as he tees up. He hits a dribbler and starts pounding a nearby bush with his driver.

"Chill, money," Al says. "Which is to say, relax."

"Speak English!" Jack shouts.

"Like, take a chill," Al says.

Jack turns toward Al, waving his driver in the air menacingly. Suddenly S. emerges from behind the bush.

"It's understandable that you have a plethora of anxieties," she tells Jack. "But you have to make a herculean effort to control them."

Jack, seeing the logic in that, puts the driver in his golf bag and apologizes for the outburst. "It was stupid crazy of me," he says.

What the Heck!

June 6, 1988

I READ THAT GEORGE BUSH — who, for reasons that his advisers can't fathom, comes across as this rich Eastern preppie with a sailboat — is trying to be taken for more of a regular guy. In his final primary campaign appearances, Bush seemed to say things like "The heck with it!" whenever he was in the presence of anyone who might come anywhere near qualifying as a regular guy. Once, in a drug rehabilitation center in Newark, he said to one of the residents, "Did you come here and say, 'The heck with it, I don't need this darn thing'?" I don't think that sort of talk is going to do the trick.

For one thing, regular guys don't say "The heck with it!" much. I haven't heard it in years myself, and I'm speaking as someone who — in the line of duty, of course — has been in some pretty bad bars. It's not impossible, of course, that in some waterfront saloon someplace, a longshoreman who's been shut off by the bartender late in the evening has responded by saying, just before he slings a long-neck in the direction of the Pabst Blue Ribbon decorative mirror, "Well then, the heck with it!" It's not impossible, for that matter, that a bartender who decided to serve the longshoreman after all has said, "Oh, devil take the hindmost!" It's not even impossible that earlier in the evening, when someone down the bar predicted that the Orioles were surely going to finish in the first division, the longshoreman said, "Oh, pshaw! Stuff and feathers!" Somehow, though, it doesn't sound right.

With Bush, it never sounds right. As rich Eastern preppies with sailboats go — and in the line of duty I've put in some time with them, too, most of which made me long for a bad bar somewhere — he's probably a pretty regular guy. But when it comes to regular-guy talk, he's got a tin ear. Some rich Eastern preppies with sailboats — including some who have a lot less concern with people who are not in the club than George Bush has demonstrated — can sound perfectly natural exchanging pleasantries with longshoremen. But some of them are fated to walk through life as if encased in a sort of tweedy cocoon.

Bush is one of those. A man who lived ten years in Midland, Texas, and can still remark that his Iowa supporters may have missed a straw poll because they were at their daughters' coming-out parties is a man in a cocoon. Judging from his résumé, Bush has lived among fighter pilots and oil-well roughnecks and spies, but culturally he never left the porch of the yacht club.

Whenever I read that some of Bush's advisers believe he'd do well to spend the time before the convention going around the country and mixing with real folks a bit, I just shudder. I can see him at a truck stop saying things like "How about another splash of coffee, kiddo?" I can see him at a bass-fishing tournament asking some of the contestants if they'd like to drop around campaign headquarters for a cold beer "sort of sixish."

From what we've seen of Republican presidential campaigns

in the past, a gang of regular-guy consultants will probably be brought in to get Bush prepared to meet the folks. Republicans love consultants. The regular-guy consultants will teach Bush how to dress ("Just for starters, Mr. Vice President, I think the cowboy hat and jeans would look even better with boots instead of Topsiders") and how to talk ("Yes sir, I'm sure there are a lot of people who say 'Well, I'll be a monkey's uncle,' but I think some of the phrases we've got on the computer printout there are a little more up-to-date").

I hope that for his own sake Bush eventually decides to boot out the consultants. If they were the ones running for president, after all, it would be silly for them to pretend to be rich Eastern preppies with sailboats. The best thing Bush could do, I think, is to load up his sailboat with all of the paraphernalia the consultants brought to Kennebunkport — all of those feed-company baseball hats and six-packs of Lone Star — and take it all out in the harbor and dump it over the side. Then he could have himself a nice sail, after he said, "The heck with that darn stuff!"

Our Brochure

June 27, 1988

A WHILE BACK, I read in *Newsday* that guests at the Palm Beach estate of Donald Trump, the real estate tycoon and braggart, are given a brochure describing the architecture and furnishings. It never ceases to amaze me how many good ideas that man has. No wonder he's always telling everybody that he's a genius.

I told my wife that our house could be the first one in the neighborhood to have a brochure describing its architecture and furnishings. She didn't seem enthusiastic. Of course, she hadn't seemed enthusiastic several years ago when I told her that our house could be the first one in the neighborhood to have an American Hereford Association poster hanging in the hallway. Sometimes I think my wife has no serious interest in being a design pacesetter.

"Listen to the sort of thing the Trumps have in their brochure," I said to her, reading from a column by James Revson that quoted some of the descriptions. " 'From the porte cochere, one enters the hall through a massive and magnificent iron grille door.' "

"We don't have a porte cochere," my wife said.

"Is that right?" I said. "Funny, I thought for sure I saw a porte cochere around here somewhere. Did you look in the basement? You'd be amazed what I came across down there the other day when I finally got around to changing the light bulb. There are a couple of very nice three-legged folding chairs, for instance, and the box from that toaster that shorted out last year. I wouldn't be surprised if back in the corner, underneath all those Halloween costumes and the Christmas tree lights — what we might call the National Holiday Corner in the brochure, I suppose — we've got a porte cochere or two."

"A porte cochere is a gateway for carriages, leading into a courtyard," my wife said. "We don't have a gateway and we don't have a courtyard and we don't have a porte cochere."

The mere fact of not having a porte cochere is not the sort of detail that Donald Trump would allow to stand in his way if he wanted to describe his porte cochere. According to Revson, the table described in the Trumps' brochure as the most amazing piece in the dining room ("Joseph Urban designed the table, using the motifs of the antique tables in the Pitti and Uffizi Galleries in Florence . . .") is nowhere in the house. No problem. We're not talking here about a notarized list of assets. We're talking about a nice brochure to satisfy the curiosity of friends and acquaintances. It's always possible, for instance, that the UPS deliveryman might say one day, while waiting at the door for a signature, "That's a nice-looking table you've got over there, except for the way it sags a little on one end." I'd like to be able to hand him a brochure.

" 'The focal point of the main body of the house is the enormous glass arched Romanesque style window,' " I continued from the Revson column, ignoring my wife's quibble about the precise contents of our basement. " 'It is set deep in the border of carved pelicans, the glass edged with very lacy iron grille.' " I hope the actual brochure on Trump's estate isn't full of pictures of all this iron grille-work, by the way; from what Revson quotes, the place must look sort of like San Quentin.

To give my wife some idea of how brochure descriptions of our furnishings might sound, I read her the one I had already prepared on the armchair in our older daughter's bedroom: " 'This chair is generally considered the softest item of furniture in the house, except for one mattress that the owners have been meaning to replace for years. Its origins are generally thought to be a thirty-percent-off sale at Macy's in 1966, although B. Altman's has also been mentioned by some scholars. Its first reupholstering, believed to have been done in the early seventies, was destroyed by two cats in a variety of ways, most of them too distasteful to mention. It is fully paid for.' "

"Why would anyone want to read about our old armchair?" my wife said.

"Well then, maybe I should lead off with a description of the new refrigerator: 'The refrigerator is newly purchased. You'd be surprised what a new refrigerator costs these days.' "

I think it's only a matter of time until she agrees that a brochure is just what we need. I've already given a lot of consideration to what we should put on the cover. For a long time I thought it should be a picture of the American Hereford Association poster. Then it occurred to me that a color photo of my neon THIS BUD'S FOR YOU sign might make a snappier cover. We were the first in our neighborhood to have a neon THIS BUD'S FOR YOU sign.

Smart Camera

July 11, 1988

WHEN WE WERE about to take a trip to Italy, somebody offered to lend me one of those cameras that know everything. The camera knows how to focus itself. It knows when to speed itself up and when to slow itself down. It knows when to flash its flashbulb. If you point the camera at a mountain, the camera knows that it's pointed at a mountain. If you suddenly swing the camera away from the mountain, point it at your Uncle Harry, and say to the camera, "This is also a mountain," the camera is not fooled. The camera knows your Uncle Harry from a mountain. The camera knows everything.

I told my wife that I was uneasy about carrying around a camera that knows everything. There are certain things I'd just as soon keep to myself.

"The camera doesn't know everything," my wife said. "It just knows more about taking pictures than you do."

I told my wife that I was uneasy about carrying around a camera that knows more than I do. It's bad enough that both of my daughters now know more than I do. If there were a ranking done in our house according to who knows the most, at least

I'd come in a strong fourth. (We don't have a dog.) Who wants to be edged out by a camera?

My wife told me I was being silly. She said to take the camera. I finally took the camera. My wife knows more about these things than I do.

One of my daughters offered to teach me how to use the camera.

"Why do I need you to teach me?" I said. "If this camera knows everything, it can teach me itself."

My daughter told me I was being silly. So I accepted her offer. She knows more about these things than I do. She can set one of those watches that work with tiny buttons on the side and will give you the month and year and the military time in Guam if you know which buttons to push. Sometimes, if there's a lull in the conversation at the dinner table, my daughter will say, "It's eighteen hundred hours in Guam." Or at least she did until the night I responded by announcing, "All enlisted personnel are required to finish their broccoli before leaving the mess hall." That was just before she got so she knew more than I did.

So she taught me to use the camera. She read the instruction booklet — several years ago I swore off instruction booklets — and studied the camera from a number of angles. Then she taught me this: "Just press the button. The camera does the rest. The camera knows everything."

So I took the camera to Italy. The first thing I did was to point it at a mountain. Then I pressed the button. The camera seemed to know just what to do. It focused itself. It slowed itself down, or maybe speeded itself up. It decided not to use its flashbulb. When I pushed the button, it advanced itself to the next picture with a contented buzzing sound, like a horsefly that has just had a bite of something good.

I felt proud of my camera. "Hey, this camera knows everything," I told my wife.

"Let's hope so," my wife said.

Just to make sure, I pointed the camera at my wife and said to it, "This is my Uncle Harry." But the camera knew better. I could tell by the contented buzz. The camera took a picture of my wife. The camera knows everything.

So I started taking a lot of pictures. I took the usual kinds of pictures — shadows falling in quaint piazzas and fishermen unloading their catch and Americans slapping themselves in the head when a waiter in a café tells them how much their two beers and a Coke cost.

The camera buzzed and buzzed. Pretty soon I was so accustomed to the buzzing that I thought I could detect not just the camera's mood but what it was trying to say. When I took a picture of an old market-vendor selling onions, I thought I heard the camera say, "Nice shot!"

Then, as I was taking a picture of a raggedy little boy talking to a splendidly dressed policeman, I thought I heard the camera say, "Cor-ny, cor-ny." That afternoon, when I was taking a picture of my wife in front of a statue of Zeus, I clearly heard the camera say, "You're cutting off his head, dummy."

So I quit using the camera. I told my wife I had run out of film. She suggested I buy some. "If the camera's so smart," I said, "let it buy its own film."

Family Entertainment

August 22, 1988

LET'S SAY that there was this family that had been loaned a VCR and was talking about which video movies to rent. Let's say this happened in August, when the family was staying in an old house in the country that is miles from the nearest movie theater and doesn't get TV reception unless you're willing to install a dish the size of a small upended hockey rink. Let's not mention any names.

The discussion was not going well at first, because the Older Daughter and the Younger Daughter kept sighing when the Father said how nice it would be to see *Casablanca* a few times. Then the Father presented the family with a good idea about how to decide which movies to rent. The Father has a lot of good ideas, no matter what people say.

Here was the Father's idea: avoid compromise. The mistake families make in these situations, he said, is to try to find movies that are minimally acceptable to everyone in the family. The thing to do, the Father said, was to take turns choosing movies.

The person whose turn it was would have complete control of the evening's entertainment, even if that person happened to be the Younger Daughter, a connoisseur of teenage-heartthrob movies who would cheerfully watch a training film for insulation installers if it had Rob Lowe in it.

The Younger Daughter thought that was a good idea, since she didn't see any other way she was going to get teenage-heartthrob movies in the house. "Like fresh, Pops," she said — or words to that effect.

The Older Daughter didn't say much of anything. The only movie she had any interest in seeing was *Room with a View*, a sensitive love story that she had seen twenty-eight times, and she already knew it wasn't available on video at the nearby general store.

The Mother, who liked foreign movies, looked skeptical. She knew that the Father was completely intolerant when it came to movies. He refused to go to anything he considered a "sissy movie," a category in which he included all sensitive love stories and "any foreign-language movie that doesn't have a car chase." The only time he had ever seen a teenage-heartthrob movie was on an airplane — he had often said that he would watch anything on an airplane — and the stewardess had to warn him that his earphones would be confiscated if he didn't quit disturbing the other passengers by booing and shouting, "Gimme a break!"

"Of course, we'd have to set some ground rules," the Father said.

"Uh-oh," the Older Daughter said. "Here it comes."

"I was simply going to say that we naturally have to rule out movies with subtitles," the Father said.

"You mean that on the night it's your turn to choose the movie you're not going to choose a movie with subtitles," the Mother said. "You're going to choose a movie with Cary Grant and Audrey Hepburn or a movie where a lot of people get shot off horses."

"No, I mean that on that tiny screen subtitles are obviously not advisable," the Father said.

"This sounds suspiciously like a ban on sissy movies to me," the Mother said.

"Well, I certainly didn't think the day would come when I was the only person concerned with the eyesight of members of this family," the Father said.

"The subtitles wouldn't be any danger to your eyes, Daddy," the Older Daughter said, "because you always fall asleep anyway."

"Also," the Father said, "I don't think we should allow movies about a new boy who moves to town and, being a kind of maverick, isn't really accepted by the cool kids in the high school, including the most popular girl and, particularly, her boyfriend, a large football player who is openly hostile to the new boy, who, in fact, eventually triumphs over the boyfriend and becomes the coolest guy of all and also, of course, wins the heart of the most popular girl."

"What!" the Younger Daughter said. "But you promised!"

"I've already seen that movie," the Father said. "I saw it on an airplane."

"You didn't see it on an airplane, because they took your earphones away," the Mother said.

"I saw enough of it to know the plot," the Father said.

"Don't bother to set a ground rule about not seeing movies

that have 'room' or 'view' in the title," the Older Daughter said. "It's not at the store anyway."

"I have a better idea," the Mother said. "Why don't we rent movies that are minimally acceptable to everybody."

"Well, O.K., if that's the way you want to do it," the Father said. "We can start with *Casablanca.*"

Summer Projects

September 5, 1988

WASN'T THIS THE SUMMER you were going to learn Spanish? Oh. Well, no need to explain. I was just asking. No big deal. I know you must have had a lot on your hands, what with clearing away that brush you said you were finally going to get rid of.

Oh. Well, I understand completely. It was really terribly hot this summer. A lot of professional brush cutters probably took the summer off. And I bet not one of them learned Spanish. There's really no need to apologize. It's not as if it were my brush. And there's certainly no hurry. I'm sure it'll be there next summer. There aren't a lot of brush thieves in this part of the world. Even if there were, of course, they'd be doing you a favor.

This sure wasn't the sort of summer anyone would want to be out there clearing brush. With the heat we had I don't blame you for wanting to confine your exercise to something completely mental. Now that I think of it, weren't you going to have a project this summer of looking up, once and for all, the answers to all those summer questions your kids are always stumping you with? I thought that was a great idea. "What a dad!" I said to my wife when you told me about that. "His plan is to get some books out of the library and really find out what causes tides and why evergreen trees stay green and what the difference is between a small continent and a large island."

I want to tell you again how much I admired that. Also, I must admit, I was running out of answers myself. For years, when the kids asked me about tides I just said, "It's sort of like a big bathtub. Just think of a bathtub, when you move back and forth and the water swooshes from one end to the other." And then just this summer one of the kids said, "O.K., the water in the ocean swooshes like the water in a bathtub, but what makes it swoosh? Is there a big huge person moving back and forth on the bottom?"

Well, I admit I had to change the subject slightly. I said, "If you don't keep those sneakers tied, we're not going to the beach at all next summer, so you won't have to worry about the tides." But it occurred to me that by this fall you'd have the answers to all of those questions stored up, and I could sort of borrow them — giving full credit, of course. So what is the answer to that one about the tides? I mean, I know the idea of a big huge person is not something a grown-up would believe. For instance, if there were a big huge person treating the ocean like a bathtub, just think of the size of the rubber ducky in there with him. That's just silly. I didn't give that a thought, really. But what does make the water swoosh?

Oh. Well I guess those books would have been hard to find anyway. You know, some of the information you'd think would be easy to find in the library — kept on a special shelf right there near the door, maybe, the way supermarkets have cigarettes and those trashy newspapers right at the cash register

— turns out to be pretty hard to put your hands on. Also, I guess during the summer books on tides are likely to be checked out pretty much all the time.

And I think it's good, in the long run, for kids to find out the answers to those questions themselves, instead of having Dad right there to tell them just exactly why the water swooshes back and forth. Teach them the value of a little digging. I'll bet if somebody had just furnished you all the answers on a silver platter, you wouldn't have turned out to be the sort of person who resolved to get all the way through Henry Kissinger's memoirs this summer. And I have to tell you this: I really respect that. I respect a person who absolutely insists on being a well-informed citizen. How'd that Kissinger book go, anyway? Did he talk about what effect bombing Cambodia had on his lecture fees at all, or was it mostly that policy stuff?

Oh. Well. I think most of the important information was probably in the first twenty pages anyway. Those guys know how to pack a lot right up at the front for the reviewers. Never mind. I don't think Kissinger speaks Spanish himself, by the way. No problem. Listen, there's plenty of time for those things. So tell me — how was your summer?

The Quayle-Gorbachev Summit

September 26, 1988

DOUBTS ABOUT WHETHER President Dan Quayle can deal effectively with Soviet leader Mikhail Gorbachev intensified today after President Quayle interrupted his first superpower summit meeting three times in one day to phone his dad.

White House aides were quick to play down the importance of the calls, which occurred on the second day the two leaders met with no one else except their interpreters present. But few foreign-policy specialists were reassured by the White House statement that "President Quayle did what any normal world leader would do." Mr. Gorbachev did not call his dad at all.

The question of whether Dan Quayle is up to dealing with Mikhail Gorbachev has, of course, been uppermost in the minds of Washington observers ever since Mr. Quayle succeeded to office on the day George Bush resigned to take a job driving an eighteen-wheeler — a career change for Mr. Bush that was described by some as the crowning success of his effort to become a regular guy and by others as "some serious overcompensation for the wimp thing."

It is unclear how effective Mr. Bush himself would have been at a summit with Mr. Gorbachev. While he was Vice President, Mr. Bush had been given the opportunity to spend a few moments with the Soviet Premier during the Reagan-Gorbachev summit in Washington. The two men reportedly got along well, although Soviet diplomats have indicated that Mr. Gorbachev remains puzzled by what the then Vice President said to him: "Hi, guy. Where'd you prep?"

There is now some speculation in Washington, though, that the Bush resignation was brought on partly by the approach of the summit. Apparently, what began as a simple habit Mr. Bush had of emphasizing his common touch by dropping the *g* at the end of *ing* words when talking to blue-collar audiences ("He's a liberal comin' out of nowhere") had been carried to the point of becoming a serious impediment to communication.

The progressive nature of Mr. Bush's habit was first noticed in a speech on September 6, 1988, to a factory audience in Oregon. In talking about the effect of inflation on personal savings, he said that inflation could eat up "a guy's savin' " — dropping not only a *g* but also an *s*. People who worked in the Bush White House now say that the reason Mr. Bush almost never spoke in public during the last few weeks of his Administration was that the letter-dropping had gradually progressed, letter by letter, to the point at which he would have had to face Mr. Gorbachev with a limited number of consonants at his disposal.

Whatever the reason for Mr. Bush's resignation, there was widespread feeling in Washington that it should have meant the postponement of this summit. Mr. Quayle was faced not only with the sudden assumption of the burdens of the presidency but also with a number of rumors in Washington that we now know were not true. Apparently, the wealthy Indiana newspaper family that Mr. Quayle comes from did not, in fact, arrange for the trucking job that supposedly lured Mr. Bush from the White House, although the "two or three routine calls" they acknowledge making may have had something to do with his getting the coveted Worcester-Spartenburg run. Apparently, the Russian ambassador to the United Nations did not ask his American counterpart, "What does it mean in English when it's said someone 'doesn't have a whole lot upstairs'?"

Many senators and representatives, on both sides of the aisle, believe that it was a mistake for Mr. Quayle to attend a summit conference while doubts still persisted about whether he had the stature and ability to negotiate head-to-head with Mikhail Gorbachev. Even before Mr. Quayle left the capital, the line most quoted in Washington gathering spots about the summit was the observation of one Foreign Policy Committee aide that "our only chance is that Gorbachev gets suspended for using anabolic steroids."

What concerns American observers at the summit about the calls to the senior Quayle is the possibility that they were not, in fact, calls for advice or assistance. Some people see the calls as confirmation of a disturbing rumor regarding the still-secret summit negotiations. They believe that Mr. Quayle may be trying to explain to his family how, after the first day of one-on-one discussions, Gorbachev somehow ended up not only with Alaska but also with controlling interest in the *Indianapolis Star*.

Costume Planning

October 17, 1988

THOSE WHO PERSIST in thinking that I don't take enough interest in my wardrobe are apparently not aware of how much effort goes into the selection of my Halloween costume. Most years I begin preliminary planning in August.

"Do you think I've overdone my ax murderer's mask?" I asked my wife this August as she sat on the dock late on a sunny afternoon reading a book. "Don't be afraid to say so if that's the way you feel. I want you to be absolutely honest about this."

"Mmmm," my wife said, apparently thinking I had said something about how the wind seemed to be coming up a bit.

"I was asking about my ax murderer's mask for Halloween," I said. "Do you think I've overdone it?"

"You ask me that every August," my wife said, without looking up from her book.

"Well, it's always nice to have family traditions," I said. It's true that my Halloween costume planning often begins with a discussion of my ax murderer's mask. In our neighborhood we have a big costume parade on Halloween, and after annual discussions about the advantages of adopting an entirely new look, I do often end up parading in my ax murderer's mask. I love my ax murderer's mask. But the mask itself is certainly not my entire costume. Every year I have to select what I suppose you might call the accessories.

"Did you think that old bathrobe was a good addition last year?" I asked my wife. Last Halloween I wore my ax murderer's mask, a baseball hat that had on the front the name SOUTH BROOKLYN CASKET COMPANY and a picture of a casket, an old bathrobe, and, fastened to my forearm, an extremely realistic rubber lizard. I've been wearing the baseball hat for a couple of years now — it was a gift from my friend Fred, who moved from New York to Maryland, where he didn't think he'd need it — and I've always worn the lizard. But the bathrobe was a new touch last year.

"Actually, a lot of people didn't quite understand that costume," my wife said. "They asked me what exactly you were supposed to be."

"I was supposed to be an ax murderer who works in a casket factory and likes to walk around in an old bathrobe with a lizard on his arm," I said. "And I thought I was rather convincing in the role."

Also, it turned out that nobody else in the parade had thought of going in that particular costume. During the weeks before Halloween, people in our neighborhood kind of feel one another out about costumes — "What are you going as?" is the normal greeting on the street — but it's still possible to spend months working on your killer-bee costume and then show up Halloween night to find that you're not the only killer bee in the crowd. You might spot someone who, with accompaniment from a built-in tape deck, is doing a pretty good imitation of a killer bee mamboing up from South America. Someone else is there as a killer bee whose wings make your wings look kind of stumpy. Two or three people are doing killer bees as celebrities — what Bette Midler would look like as a killer bee, maybe, or a killer bee as Kurt Waldheim. There are twenty-five people from an aerobics class costumed as a swarm of killer bees. You feel a little bit like going home and getting into the Oscar the Grouch costume you wore the year before.

I know how I'd feel if I showed up one year to find all sorts of people costumed as an ax murderer who works in a casket factory and likes to walk around in a bathrobe with a lizard on his arm. Actually, that's one of the possibilities I tend to discuss with my wife in August.

"You don't think I might have spawned a lot of imitators, do you?" I asked her this summer.

"I think you can put your mind at rest on that score," she said.

She was probably right. Still, there was a great temptation to take a completely fresh approach with my costume — to go to the parade as a butter churn, say, or as Woodrow Wilson. I knew there would be risks in that. We all admired my friend Ernie's ambition when he decided to go as "The March of the Toy Soldiers," for instance, but we all thought his costume simply demonstrated that the concept was too much for one person to carry off alone.

"I think I might stick with the ax murderer's mask and the same accessories, if that's the way you feel," I said to my wife. "Of course, this is only preliminary."

"Mmmm," my wife said.

In Support of Quayle

October 11, 1988

I SUPPOSE MY CAMPAIGN for a Constitutional amendment that would make a C average a requirement for the presidency was bound to be seen as an attack on Dan Quayle.

That's certainly the way my Aunt Rosie saw it. She phoned from Kansas City the minute she read about my proposal for the Twenty-seventh Amendment: "No person shall be eligible for the Office of President who has not maintained a C average in the highest educational institution that such person attended, including institutions that such person bought his way into."

"I'm surprised at the way you've been picking on that poor boy," Aunt Rosie said. "I know very well you weren't raised to make fun of people who are a little slow."

I tried to defend myself against Aunt Rosie's criticism — speaking, of course, with the respect and deference I always show older relatives. "You're getting to be a particularly soft-hearted old bat, Aunt Rosie," I said. "What are you, some kind of liberal?"

"How do you think it makes the poor boy's children feel when you keep describing their father as not having 'a whole lot upstairs'?" Aunt Rosie said.

"I thought it might make them feel good to be reminded how simple it's going to be to snooker him out of the family car," I said, trying to look on the bright side for a change.

"And don't think I didn't read that column where you said that J. Danforth Quayle sounded like the name of the rich banker in Donald Duck comics," Aunt Rosie said. "Since when do you go around ridiculing people's names?"

"Well, he didn't have any obvious physical disability I could make fun of," I said. "Any port in a storm."

Even as I defended myself, though, I realized that Aunt Rosie's criticism had made me feel uneasy. People assume that those of us who make our livings as jackals of the press pack, snarling and snapping at citizens who have chosen to devote themselves to public service, have no feelings at all. Not true. Almost true, but not true.

"Why can't you find something good to say about him?" Aunt Rosie went on. "And I don't mean something like that remark about how people who went to DePauw say he was 'definitely not the dumbest guy in the Deke house.' I know very well you didn't mean that as a compliment."

"I resent that, Aunt Rosie," I said. "You happen to be talking about my best effort at balanced coverage."

But as much as I might have argued the matter with Aunt Rosie, in a respectful way ("I'm beginning to think you've been nipping at the Pink Catawba again, Aunt Rosie"), I knew she had a point there. That remark about where Dan Quayle ranked in intelligence among his college fraternity brothers doesn't really stand up under the test of what qualifies as a compliment.

I had to admit, when I thought about it, that I couldn't imagine a Republican campaign placard that said VOTE FOR DAN QUAYLE — DEFINITELY NOT THE DUMBEST GUY IN THE DEKE HOUSE.

"The worst thing," Aunt Rosie went on in her sternest tones, "is that you want him to win so you'll have him around to make fun of for the next four years."

Innocent! Oh, I'll admit that at the beginning Quayle looked good for us jackals. We saw it all there before us: Spoiled rich kid jokes. Shirker jokes. Dumb Deke jokes. Airhead jokes. Right-wing wacko family jokes. We saw an awful lot there that we like in a public official.

But that feeling of euphoria didn't last long. First, I realized that Quayle's name was cropping up more and more in the monologues of lounge comics. Then a traveling salesman of my acquaintance asked me if I had heard of the Quayle war movie *(Thirty Seconds over Indianapolis)* and the Quayle war song ("Over Here"). Our kids started bringing Quayle jokes home from high school. People began putting Quayle jokes on their answering machines. Weeks before the end of the campaign, in other words, Dan Quayle had become the equivalent of knock-knock jokes. I realized then that Quayle was not going to be of much use to people like me. We can't be in the position of asking for money (even the small coin they toss our way) for telling the same sorts of jokes that every bartender hands out free along with a paper napkin and a dish of peanuts.

"I'm innocent, Aunt Rosie," I said, explaining that by the time of the inauguration, telling jokes about Dan Quayle would be like telling jokes about Howard Cosell or Vanna White (except that they don't happen to be in the line of succession to the presidency). "Or as innocent as I get."

Checking the Spell-Check

November 7, 1988

MY SPELL-CHECK doesn't understand me. I'll admit that it does everything the instructions for my word-processing program claim it will do. When I command it to go over what I've written, it stops to highlight any word that can't be found in its supply of one hundred thousand correctly spelled words. When it does that, it offers an array of correctly spelled words close enough to the mangled word so that one of them might have been what I had in mind. It does all this without shaking its head in frustration the way my fourth-grade teacher, Miss McCardle, used to shake her head in frustration when she was my spell-check.

That's all just fine. I appreciate it. And I certainly appreciate the fact that my spell-check, unlike Miss McCardle, never says anything like "Are you sure you don't need some extra help?" Still, my spell-check doesn't understand me.

Some of the words that stop my spell-check aren't misspelled at all; they're just words I use that are unfamiliar to my spell-check. This never happened with Miss McCardle. I might as well admit that when I was in fourth grade I used some words that were presumably unfamiliar to Miss McCardle, but that was out on the playground. If she had heard those particular words, she would have done more than offer an array of correctly spelled words that I might have had in mind.

But my spell-check sees all the words I use. Take the word "wacko." My spell-check is always stopped by "wacko." My spell-check thinks I mean wacky or waxy or wick or whelk or wok or walkway. I don't. I mean wacko, as in "The White House is leaning heavily on the advice of some wacko who believes devoutly in the economic theories of the late Adolph Menjou" or "It's being whispered that at least one high official in Meese's Justice Department is not a wacko, although if the word ever got out he could presumably lose his job." How could my spell-check expect me to get through eight years of the Reagan Administration without the word "wacko"?

A computer-freak friend of mine told me that I could train my spell-check not to stop at any unusual but correctly spelled word that I intended to use a lot. He said that there's a way to add, say, the word "wacko" to the words the spell-check already knows, so that it wouldn't always get the impression that I was trying to call someone in the Justice Department a walkway. "You can simply inform the spell-check," he said.

"It's none of the spell-check's business," I said.

I don't trust the spell-check. When the spell-check stops at one of my correctly spelled words, I can somehow hear the voice of Miss McCardle. That would be irritating even if Miss McCardle had not had a particularly irritating voice. Let's say that

I make a glancing reference to a talk-show host discussing the meaning of life with "some ditsy starlet." My spell-check stops at "ditsy." It doesn't say anything out loud. It just highlights the word in yellow and offers me what it calls, in a palpably insincere pass at giving me the benefit of the doubt, "alternate spellings." But I can hear the voice of Miss McCardle.

"Maybe you mean dizzy here," Miss McCardle says, with a condescending little smile.

"No, I don't mean dizzy," I mumble at the machine. "She might also be dizzy, but mainly she's ditsy."

"Perhaps dozy, duets, or diets," I can hear Miss McCardle saying, in a voice that somehow has grown even more nasal over the years.

"No, not dozy, duets, or diets," I say. "There's no such thing as a duets starlet. Ditsy."

"Doze or daze?" she continues.

"I don't have to listen to you, Miss McCardle," I say, astonishing myself with my boldness. "Doze daze — I mean, those days — are over."

"Bobby Carpenter would never misspell dizzy," Miss McCardle says, referring to the spelling-bee winner in my fourth-grade class. "And Bobby Carpenter would never be disrespectful to his teacher."

"You're absolutely right he wouldn't," I say, "because Bobby Carpenter was a wonk."

I get the impression that this ends the discussion on an upbeat and forthright note, but then when I spell-check what I've written, the spell-check stops at "wonk."

It highlights the word in yellow, and as I read the alternate spellings I can hear the voice of Miss McCardle going on and on.

"You must mean wink," Miss McCardle says. "Or maybe won or winch."

"Get lost, Miss McCardle," I say. "And take your spell-check with you."

"Or wince," Miss McCardle goes on. "Or whence. Or walkway."

Visitor in the Night

November 14, 1988

"WAKE UP, GEORGE," the figure standing in the shadows said. "It's time we had a little chat."

George stirred.

"Wake up, George," the visitor persisted.

George opened one eye. "It can't be the radio alarm clock," he said out loud. "Because my radio alarm is permanently set on a country music station — anybody who thinks I'm not a regular guy can check that out — and that voice is not a country voice."

"Good for you, George," the visitor said, in a voice that was indeed a voice that could belong only to an Easterner of the landed class. The words barely escaped from jaws that were almost clenched shut, as if the speaker were feeling the effects of having eaten his way through a case of Skippy chunk-style. "Marvelous. You're absolutely right. This is not one of your hayseed friends."

George sat up in bed. "Who are you?" he demanded. "What are you doing here?"

"But surely you remember, George," the visitor said. "We

made a little arrangement. You said you'd sell your very soul to win, I said that could be arranged, we shook on it, and that was that. A handshake between gentlemen."

"But I didn't make that deal with you," George said. "I made it with Roger Ailes, my media adviser. You don't look like Roger Ailes."

"You must know, George, that I can appear in any form I choose to appear in," the visitor said. "And, not to be snobbish about it, the form of Roger Ailes is not actually one of my favorites."

George reached over for his glasses. He tried to focus on the visitor, who was still standing in the shadows, almost enfolded in the heavy bedroom drapes. "But you look familiar," George said to the visitor. "Where'd you prep?"

"You're getting warm, George."

George stared at the visitor. Then he said, tentatively, "Coach Watson?"

"An old enemy of mine," the visitor said. "I took his face this evening as a little joke."

"Coach Watson is the one who taught me that when the Great Scorekeeper comes around he doesn't ask who won or lost but how they played the game," George said. "Coach Watson told me that winning a game was worthless if you had to stick your thumb in a man's eye to do it."

"I don't know why people persist in saying that you've gone through life remembering names and forgetting lessons," the visitor said. "Those were precisely Watson's lessons — the old fool."

"But Roger said I was just doing what I had to do," George said.

"They didn't bring you up to do what you had to do, George," the visitor said. "They brought you up to do what you were supposed to do."

Suddenly George felt very cold. He pulled the covers up over his shoulders, wrapping himself in them as he had learned to do with the flag. "Listen," he said. "I could have won anyway. I didn't need Willie Horton or the ACLU thing. We had peace and prosperity on our side. We had the South."

"Watson could have won the Exeter game anyway," the visitor said. "But when I presented him with the opportunity to distract the Exeter quarterback with a young lady of my acquaintance, just to be on the safe side, he threw me out of his office."

George was silent for a while. Finally he said, "I don't know how to ask this exactly, but you don't have any plans to — you know — well, call in the bet right away, do you? If you know what I mean." He wrapped the blankets more tightly around his shoulders, but a shiver went through him.

"Are you kidding!" the visitor said. "Considering the airhead who'd succeed you if I did! Listen, I may change forms all the time, but I've got to live in this country."

Suddenly George heard another voice — singing. "I ain't bowlin' in your bowlin' league no more," the voice sang. "You bowled a strike when it came to me, but now we're split and I can see: you used me as a spare, though it really wasn't fair. Then you told me as you left me at the door that I ain't bowlin' in your bowlin' league no more."

The clock alarm! "Country music," George muttered as he opened his eyes. "See. I told you it's set to country music." He looked toward the drapes. The visitor seemed to be fading. "It was all a dream," George said.

"For you, maybe," the visitor said, in a voice growing fainter. "The rest of us are going to have to live through it."

Canada Was Famous

November 28, 1988

CANADA WAS FAMOUS for fifteen minutes. There has to be something wrong with that. When Andy Warhol said that someday everyone would be famous for fifteen minutes, he was talking about people, not entire countries. Canada is, by land mass, the second-largest country in the world. That should be good for at least half an hour.

Canada got famous for fifteen minutes during its national parliamentary elections, mainly because the issue in the elections was whether to sign a free-trade agreement with the United States, a country that is permanently famous to the point of distraction.

Canadians have been arguing for a year about whether to sign the free-trade agreement because some of them think it would lead to increasing domination of Canada by the United States. Americans, the people assigned by the agreement to do the dominating, hadn't heard about the free-trade agreement until Canada got famous. Now they've heard of it, but they don't know exactly what's in it. You can't really learn an awful lot about something like a free-trade agreement in fifteen minutes. Also, things that are famous for fifteen minutes tend to get mixed up in people's minds, so a lot of Americans think the free-trade agreement has something to do with the whales that were stuck in the ice in Alaska, or maybe Donna Rice.

Actually, you can't learn a lot about something like a free-trade agreement in a year. Even Canadians don't know everything that's in it. For instance, Canadians don't seem to realize that now that they've voted in a parliament that's going to approve the agreement, they're going to have to change their Thanksgiving Day to our Thanksgiving Day. That's right. It's implied in the fine print.

The Canadians celebrate Thanksgiving in October, on what is our Columbus Day, and they don't celebrate Columbus Day at all. Canadians think Christopher Columbus discovered the New World, but they don't care. Americans, particularly Italian-Americans, care desperately.

If the economies of Canada and the United States become more or less one economy, we can't be celebrating two different Thanksgiving Days. Think of what would happen if a customer in Winnipeg phoned a widget supplier in Pennsylvania on what the Canadian thought was an ordinary (if bitterly cold) November weekday, and nobody answered; he might have to phone all the way to Japan, where the widget will continue to be made no matter how the free-trade agreement works out. Picture the October afternoon when a Toronto branch manager says to a New York colleague named Sal Provolini, "Have a happy Turkey Day," and Provolini says, "If you pass another remark like that about Christopher Columbus, I'm going to come up there and rearrange your face."

We obviously can't change our Thanksgiving Day to the Canadian Thanksgiving Day. Americans all begin their Christmas shopping on the day after Thanksgiving, and if they started their Christmas shopping in the middle of October they'd run out of money sometime in November. The people who are hard to shop for wouldn't get any presents at all.

It may be inconvenient for Canadians to change their Thanksgiving Day to our Thanksgiving Day, but at least there wouldn't be any violence. Canadians don't have nearly as many guns as Americans do. Americans have a lot of guns, and the Americans who are hard to shop for tend to be the sort of people who don't mind using them. So the Canadians will have to change their Thanksgiving Day. Fair's fair.

Also, there's the question of the Pledge of Allegiance. Canadians don't have a Pledge of Allegiance. How do they get along without one? I wish I knew. Somehow they've managed to become known as people who take the responsibilities of citizenship seriously, vote in high numbers, and fight bravely in wars. Maybe they have a secret handshake or something.

Once free trade goes in, though, they're going to have to have a Pledge of Allegiance. For the next four years, after all, workers in all American offices and factories will be required to recite the Pledge of Allegiance every morning — that's what George Bush meant when he said he had a mandate — and it wouldn't be fair if Canadians could use that time to produce goods and services. They can use our Pledge of Allegiance. The Canadians who opposed the free-trade agreement might argue that if Canadians say our Pledge of Allegiance every morning they could turn into the sort of people who shoot each other with cheap pistols and have a compulsion to interfere in the internal affairs of small Latin American countries. Too bad. Fair's fair.

Anyway, if that happened, it would be news and Canada would be famous again. This time they might get twenty minutes.

Losing at Hardball

December 12, 1988

SO HERE WE HAVE F. Ross Johnson, the chief executive officer of RJR Nabisco. First he tries to buy the company for a lot less than it's worth — an attempt at snookering the very stockholders whose interests he has pledged to represent. Then it turns out that the proposed deal would enrich Johnson and his pals in a way that stuns even his own board of directors, a collection of gentlemen who themselves do not lack experience in the art of living high off someone else's hog. Then he's outmaneuvered by a bunch of Wall Street money fiddlers who three weeks before this didn't know an Oreo from a Hydrox — revealing himself to be not just greedy but ineptly greedy, like a burglar who's caught because he couldn't stand to leave before he finished off every pint of chocolate chip ice cream in the freezer. And what fate befalls F. Ross Johnson for stumbling into a debacle of truly Edsel-like proportions? He gets a booby prize of thirty-five million dollars. And they call this stuff hardball.

You'd think that in hardball F. Ross Johnson would be lucky to walk away with the clothes he was wearing — and not even all of those if he happened to have purchased the fancy Italian shoes on an RJR Nabisco expense account that time in Milan when the shoelace in the black wingtips snapped just hours before he had to be at an important meeting. In that case he'd be stopped at the door by a security man. "Sorry about this, Mr. Johnson," the security man would say as Johnson hands over the shoes, "but we got our orders."

During this entire drama, after all, we're being told that the fight for RJR Nabisco is fueled by the egos of the players, big plungers who are fiercely proud of their reputations for being willing to risk all on one roll of the dice. And what happens if they roll snake eyes? Here's a hint: it's not the same thing that happened when you rolled snake eyes in Las Vegas that time you took a flyer on one roll, figuring that, if worst came to worst, you could get next month's mortgage money rustled up some other way. It doesn't end abruptly, with someone saying "Tough luck, buddy" and the stone-faced croupier pushing the dice over to the next sucker.

What happens when one of the big-ego risk-takers risks all and comes up with snake eyes is that the croupier sighs and says, "Oh, that's really a pity."

The high roller just stands there, his lower lip quivering. The floor manager comes over and puts his arm around the high roller's shoulder.

"Look, it's not the end of the world," the floor manager says. "Cheer up. When we say 'all' we don't necessarily mean absolutely every itty-bitty eensy-weensy bit. What if we gave you just a few million so you could buy yourself some Burger King franchises? Would that make you feel better? There now — give us a little smile. That's better. Just stop at the booby prize window on your way out."

I'm sorry I missed the conversation among Johnson and his directors which resulted in the establishment of a thirty-five-million-dollar golden parachute. Don't forget: the high rollers speak only in terms of what they're doing for the stockholders. If the managers of RJR Nabisco run the sort of romantic cigarette advertisements that encourage young people to take up a habit that might well kill them, it's only because management owes it to the stockholders to protect their investment. The reason the Wall Street money fiddlers who outmaneuvered poor Johnson were interested in the deal was not because it would generate millions for buying stretch limos and hiring press agents to get their names in the gossip columns and making donations that allow them to mingle at charity balls with people they consider their social betters; their announced motive was to "maximize value for shareholders."

So before all of this started, F. Ross Johnson must have said to the chairman of the board, "How do you think the stockholders feel about me?"

"They love you, F.," the chairman says. "They figure you're not the kind of guy who's going to worry about what the palm oil in the cookies does to arteries as long as it prolongs shelf life — because your only concern is protecting their investment."

"How are the stockholders going to feel if I ever mess up so badly I have to be shown the door?" Johnson says.

"They're going to feel awful," the chairman says, "because they love you, big guy."

"Maybe they'd feel better if they gave me, say, fifty million."

"Let's make it thirty-five," the chairman says. "After all, this is hardball."

A Fruitcake Theory

December 19, 1988

THIS WAS THE YEAR I was going to be nice about fruitcake. "Just try to be nice," my wife said. My younger daughter — the one who is still in high school and talks funny — said the same thing. Actually, what she said was, "Cool it, Pops. Take a chill on the fruitcake issue." That's the same thing.

They were right. I knew they were right. It's not that I hadn't tried to be nice before. It's not my fault that some years ago I happened to pass along a theory about fruitcake I had heard from someone in Denver. The theory was that there is only one fruitcake, and that this fruitcake is simply sent on from year to year. It's just a theory.

But every year around this time, someone calls up and says something like, "I'm doing a story on people who make fun of the holiday symbols that so many Americans hold dear — symbols that do so much for warm family life in this great country of ours and remain so very meaningful to all decent people. You're the one who maligns fruitcake, right?"

"Well, it's just a theory," I always mutter. "Something someone in Denver said once."

Who in Denver? Well, I can't remember. I'm always hearing theories from people in Denver. People in Denver are stinky with theories. I don't know why. It may be because of the altitude, although that's just a theory.

Anyway, I can't be expected to remember the name of every single person in Denver who ever laid a theory on me. I've had people in Denver tell me that if you play a certain Rolling Stones record backward you can get detailed instructions on how to dismantle a 1977 Volkswagen Rabbit. A man I once met in a bar in Denver told me that the gases produced by the drying of all these sun-dried tomatoes were causing the earth to wobble on its axis in a way that will put every pool table in the western hemisphere nearly a bubble off level by the end of this century. Don't get me started on people in Denver and their theories.

The point is that nobody ever interviews the person who gave me the theory about fruitcake, because nobody wants to start picking through this gaggle of theory-mongers in Denver to find him. So I was the one called up this year by someone who said he was doing a piece about a number of Scrooge-like creatures who seemed to derive sadistic pleasure out of trashing some of our most treasured American holiday traditions.

"Well, come right over," I said. "It's always nice to be included."

He said he'd catch me the next afternoon, just after he finished interviewing a guy who never passes a Salvation Army Santa Claus without saying, "Hiya, lard-gut."

When he arrived, I remembered that I was going to try to take a chill on the fruitcake issue. I told him that the theory about there being only one fruitcake actually came from somebody in Denver, maybe the same guy who talked to me at length about his theory that dinosaurs became extinct because they couldn't adapt to the personal income tax.

Then, trying for a little historical perspective, I told him about a family in Michigan I once read about that brings out an antique fruitcake every Christmas, a fruitcake that for some reason was not eaten at Christmas dinner in 1895 and has symbolized the holidays ever since. They put it on the table, not as dessert but as something between an icon and a centerpiece. "It's a very sensible way to use a fruitcake," I said. I was trying to be nice.

"You mean you think that fruitcake would be dangerous to eat?" he asked.

"Well, you wouldn't eat an antique," I said. "My Uncle Ralph used to chew on an old sideboard now and then, but we always considered it odd behavior."

"Would a fruitcake that isn't an antique be dangerous?"

"You mean a reproduction?"

"I mean a modern fruitcake."

"There's nothing dangerous about fruitcakes as long as people send them along without eating them," I said, in the nicest sort of way. "If people ever started eating them, I suppose there might be need for federal legislation."

"How about people who buy fruitcakes for themselves?" he asked.

"Well, now that you mention it," I said, "nobody in the history of the United States has ever bought a fruitcake for himself. People have bought turnips for themselves. People have bought any number of Brussels sprouts for themselves. But no one has ever bought a fruitcake for himself. That does tell you a little something about fruitcakes."

"Are you saying that everybody secretly hates fruitcake?" he asked.

"Well, it's just a theory."

Testing Grounds

December 26, 1988

I LIVE IN GREENWICH VILLAGE, where people from the suburbs bring their car alarms for late-night testing. "This is a test," I sometimes mutter when the whine of a car alarm wakes me up late on a Saturday night. I know that some of my neighbors must be waking up, too — the two little girls next door, and the man across the street with the funny-looking dog, and the elderly couple who live on the corner. "Don't worry — this is a test," I'd like to assure them. "I'm certain no cars are actually being stolen, because the very same cars will be back next Saturday night for the same test."

Sometimes, as I lie there in bed trying to go back to sleep, I start wondering how the suburbs produce all of these car-alarm testers. I envision a father somewhere in Westchester County sitting in his easy chair, reading his Saturday morning paper. Junior, his teenage son, walks by on his way to revel in his many material possessions.

"Son," Dad says, "have you tested the alarm on that car of yours lately?"

"Oh, Dad," the son whines, "do I have to go all the way to the Village again?"

"Remember what I told you, son," Dad says. "You take care of your car and your car will take care of you."

Meanwhile, in the suburbs of New Jersey, there's a lot of activity at the six-acre parking lot that has become the meeting place of the Bergen County Car Alarm Club. B-Ccac, as it's known, has five hundred members. Most of them spend most Saturdays fine-tuning their car alarms.

They wear identical black and gold coveralls with the club crest on the left breast pocket. The club crest shows a Pontiac with little marks coming off it, to designate sound, and people next to it holding their hands over their ears. B-Ccac members talk a lot to each other about their HTRs. An HTR is a hair-trigger response. Their goal is an HTR that will set off the alarm if the steps of one normal-size adult reverberate on the sidewalk within six feet of the car. That's called a single-person HTR. Most of the members' cars have it.

In a country club locker room in Fairfield County, Connecticut, four or five men are arguing. They are businessmen who bet a lot of money on golf games every weekend, except when it's too cold to play golf. When it's too cold to play golf, they bet on which one of their car alarms will go off faster in Greenwich Village.

They spend most of Saturday afternoon arguing about odds. The ones who have any car other than a Mercedes believe they should get odds. They believe that a Mercedes alarm is more likely to go off first because a lot of people who live in the Village have a habit of taking a kick at a Mercedes as they walk along the street — and a kick will almost certainly set off the alarm. But the people who own a Mercedes drive a hard bargain.

That's how they made enough money to buy a Mercedes in the first place.

Sometimes, as I fall asleep on Saturday night, I think of all the car-alarm testers heading my way. The teenager from Westchester and a bunch of his pals are in his car heading down the Henry Hudson Parkway, practicing some of the songs they're going to sing later in the evening to celebrate the successful testing of his car alarm. The members of the Bergen County Car Alarm Club are driving in caravan toward the George Washington Bridge. The Connecticut golfers have crossed the New York state line, still arguing on their car phones about odds.

I am about to fall asleep. But then an alarm goes off — an early arrival. I begin to wonder how long it would take to locate an alarm and turn it off, once you got inside the car. I can see myself and some neighbors trying to find out. We're holding one of those battering rams they use to knock down doors in drug busts.

The man across the street with the funny-looking dog is there, and so are the two little girls from next door and the elderly couple who live on the corner. (They are remarkably strong for their age.) Rhythmically, we're swinging the battering ram back and then against the driver's window. The window is starting to go, even though we've missed it on a couple of swings and put great dents into the door instead. Somebody in black and gold coveralls shows up and starts shouting something about whose car it is. "Don't worry," I say. "This is only a test."

Space Mess

January 2, 1989

A FEW WEEKS AGO I turned down an opportunity to worry about the litter in space. It happened when a man who was being interviewed on television said that as many as 7,200 objects, most of them the sort of thing that a good citizen might drop in the nearest trash receptacle, are orbiting the earth. Just as soon as I heard the man say that, I heard myself say, "Well, none of them belong to me."

I think you could call it an instinctive response, familiar to anyone who grew up with a sibling — a sister in my case — and thus became accustomed to using as his first line of defense "I'm not going to clean up her mess!" I wasn't denying that there's a problem. The man being interviewed said that if an astronaut who is unscrewing some little thingamajig outside the space capsule happens to drop his glove, the glove doesn't drop. It goes into orbit forever. So it stands to reason that the place needs some tidying.

To appreciate what the litter problem in space is like, all you have to do is visualize what would happen if any glove dropped right here on earth went into orbit instead of dropping. If you want to look on the bright side of that, I suppose there might be a chance of finding a lost glove of your own when it came around again, assuming it hadn't run into anything on the way, but the odds on that would be pretty long. I can't think of anything else on the bright side. The gloves lost by my children alone would be enough to turn the sky dark with gloves. You couldn't walk down the street without being pummeled by fancy silk gloves and heavy ski gloves and catcher's mitts. The sides of skyscrapers, windows and all, would be covered with layer after layer of third-graders' mittens.

So I wasn't doubting that the man on the news was talking about a genuine problem. But I thought the most honest and straightforward thing to do was to explain to him right away that I wasn't planning to treat it as my own personal problem right at that time. The way I felt about it was this: I don't expect the National Aeronautics and Space Administration to worry about my Diners Club bill, so I'm sure they don't expect me to worry about their space litter.

"After all, I didn't lose any gloves up there," I said to my wife when I was explaining to her that I wasn't going to concentrate a lot of my concern on the junk in space. "In fact, the more I think about it, the more I think that space may be the only place I've never lost a glove. If I had caused any of the litter, you know I'd be the first one trying to figure out how to get it cleaned up. But remember what my Army sergeant used to say when we were policing the general area. He said, 'The guy who dropped it is the guy who's going to pick it up.' "

"You always told me that when you were policing the general area your Army sergeant said, 'If it'll move, pick it up; if it won't move, paint it,' " my wife said.

"Well, the principle's the same," I said.

"It seems to me the principle's completely different," she said. "One way, you're responsible only for what you dropped. The other way, you're responsible for everything, whether you dropped it or not."

I realized that she was absolutely right, so I said, "You had to have been in the Army to understand."

Then I started trying to figure out what I could do about the litter in space. At just that moment, I suppose, NASA started trying to figure out what it could do about my Diners Club bill.

"I was thinking maybe we could send people up to stand on space stations with large versions of butterfly nets," I said to my wife. "On the other hand, not much of that stuff is likely to come close enough to take a swipe at. After all, there's a lot of space in space. Thus the name."

"I'd keep that idea to myself if I were you," my wife said.

"I don't suppose there'd be a practical way to put rugs in orbit to sweep it under," I said. "Also, you've got the problem of where the 'under' is in that situation."

"Maybe you shouldn't treat this as your personal problem," my wife said. "Remember what your sergeant said."

"I think you're right," I said. "When it comes right down to it, the people who have been there in space made the mess. And if they didn't, it must have been my sister."

Benefit of the Doubt

January 9, 1989

ACCORDING TO the latest survey on smoking, the percentage of smokers among people who didn't finish high school is now twice as high as among people who have graduated from college. Who says nobody is doing anything to raise the median level of education in this country? The tobacco industry seems to be on a campaign to kill off the dropouts.

I'm all for raising the education level, but you'd think that the way to bring down the dropout rate might be to give the people in question something like incentive programs or tutoring sessions rather than emphysema. I'm not even sure that this falls into the category of employing different methods to reach the same goal.

I'm going to try to look at it that way, though, because these days I'm trying to approach the news with the assumption that people may well have, at least in their own minds, good, constructive, socially useful motives for what they do. It's a sort of New Year's resolution. On New Year's Eve, I promised myself that I would assume the best of people for the entire month of January — although that doesn't apply to the President or members of Congress, of course. I wanted to reform, but there are limits.

Before my resolution, I might have assumed from this latest batch of smoking statistics that the tobacco industry, finding its customers declining among those most likely to be acquainted with the overwhelming scientific evidence linking smoking and deadly diseases, started directing its pitch toward those less likely to be familiar with such evidence — another example of the theory that when it comes to the tobacco industry, the old economic saw that applies is the one that says profits equal marketers chasing victims. That was the old me.

Now I'm reformed. The other day, for instance, I passed a billboard that was advertising cigarettes — an outdoor scene showing a couple of those absolutely beautiful and healthy-looking young smokers who can stay on a camping trail or a ski slope all day long without wrinkling their clothes. I noticed a few blurry lines in the lower right-hand corner that may or may not have been the surgeon general's warning about the risks that these invulnerable-looking young people are taking of developing lung cancer.

"It appears that anyone who wants to see that warning would have to have the sort of long-range vision usually associated with the pilot of an F-14," I said to my companion. "Perhaps the cigarette company or its advertising agency is trying to encourage regular and thorough eye examinations — an oft-stated public service message, if I'm not mistaken, of the American Ophthalmological Society."

"Have you gone soft in the head?" my companion said.

"It's also possible, of course, that the long-term goal is to play a significant role in the recovery of the American binocular industry, now in a bad way because of overseas competition."

"Why are you talking this way?" my companion said.

"Come to think of it," I said, "I now realize why cigarette companies started sponsoring golf and tennis tournaments around the time they could no longer advertise on television — because they wanted to encourage all of us to get outside in the fresh air so that every single one of us could look like their models."

My companion glanced around nervously — apparently looking for a telephone, or maybe a policeman.

"This is the new me," I explained. "At least for January, and with certain other qualifications."

In that spirit, it occurred to me that if the cigarette manufacturers want to be even more efficient in their efforts to improve the education statistics, they might ask the government to use some longer words in the surgeon general's warning — words that the average high school dropout simply wouldn't understand. If that doesn't work well enough, maybe the warning could be written in Latin.

Even as it is, according to the latest study, almost a quarter of the high school students who see cigarette advertisements don't even notice the surgeon general's warning, let alone read it. I suppose that teaches the same lesson taught by those tough outdoor courses that seek to make hardier, more resourceful citizens out of our young people — Stay Alert to Survive.

On the other hand, I have a certain affection for the sort of high school student who would take no more notice of a sober little warning off in the corner of an ad than he would of a sign that says the motel swimming pool shouldn't be used when there's no lifeguard on duty. Come to think of it, I have a certain affection for a number of people who didn't finish high school. I'll be happy when January's over.

Lucky Numbers

January 16, 1989

RONALD AND NANCY REAGAN will now be living in the Bel Air section of Los Angeles, at what used to be 666 St. Cloud Drive. I read in the newspaper that the Reagans — who, as we all know, are just a tiny bit superstitious — arranged to have the address changed because in the Bible 666 is the number of the Devil. So their house's new address will be 668 St. Cloud Drive. That's all O.K., except now where's the Devil supposed to live?

You say it's silly of me to worry about housing for the Devil because the Devil doesn't actually exist? If the Devil doesn't actually exist, why are the Reagans changing their address?

It's true that in the high-rent district of Manhattan there's a well-known office building called 666 Fifth Avenue. The Devil could live there — I would assume that he spends a lot of time in Manhattan anyway — but I think of 666 Fifth Avenue as more of a business address than a home. It happens to be a particularly unattractive building; when it first went up, twenty-five or thirty years ago, someone said it looked like the box the Seagram's Building came in. I suppose if anybody at the time had thought to ask the architect why he chose to erect such a weird-looking structure, he might have said, "The Devil made me do it."

I realize that all of this is not the sort of thing that concerns President Reagan. He's never seemed particularly alarmed about people sleeping on the streets, so he's not likely to spend a lot of his retirement time worrying about where the Prince of Darkness lays his head. John Cardinal O'Connor of New York asked Reagan the other day about criticism that his Administration had made virtually no effort at all to build housing for the homeless. This was when the President was a guest on the Cardinal's television show — just before receiving an award in New York from the Knights of Malta of America, which was described in the newspaper as an organization "dedicated to serving the sick and the poor." Reagan explained to the Cardinal that most of the people who live on the street are there because they prefer that way of life. A couple of days before Reagan spoke to the Cardinal, he told another interviewer that whatever piddling discrimination still exists against black Americans is caused partly by the fact that black civil rights leaders prefer it that way so they can remain in the spotlight.

It must be comforting to have such certainty that anyone who seems to be suffering while you thrive is suffering because he wants to be. I wouldn't have thought, though, that it was the sort of attitude that could get you an award from an organization devoted to serving the poor, particularly if you're someone who gives virtually nothing to charity and is fond of answering any question about people on the dole by one more telling of the story about the woman in California who picks up her welfare check in a Cadillac.

On the other hand, maybe the Knights were just trying to be

patriotic: citizens who do manage to convince themselves that homeless people prefer to be homeless must find it easier to follow President Reagan's parting advice about teaching our children to guard against the erosion of that high morale and optimistic American spirit that he is so proud of building during his administration. With the Reagan attitude toward the poor, the typical American family he was always talking about would have no problem at all with the otherwise inconvenient fact that these days a stroll down a typical American Main Street so often requires stepping around someone trying to sleep on a grate:

"Why are those people sleeping on a piece of cardboard over a grate, Mommy?"

"They like to sleep on the street, dear. They prefer that sort of lifestyle."

"They like sleeping on a piece of cardboard?"

"That's right, dear. Some people prefer being the sort of people whose friends buy them two-and-a-half-million-dollar houses in Bel Air, and other people prefer being the sort of people who sleep on pieces of cardboard over a grate. It's up to them, because remember what the President said in his farewell address: 'America is freedom.' "

"But isn't sleeping on the street cold and nasty and scary, Mommy?"

"Oh, no. Not at all. I was a little concerned about them yesterday, when I noticed that they were sleeping over a grate at 13 Main Street. We all know that 13 is a very unlucky number. But I notice that they've moved to a grate in front of 17 Main Street. No need to worry about them now. They'll be just fine."

Remember This Name

January 23, 1989

A WEEKLY NEWSPAPER called the *New York Observer* recently did a survey indicating that Donald Trump has ninety-four percent name recognition in New York. "Hey, I'm very flattered," Trump told the *Observer* when he was informed of the results. "But I'm just wondering who the other people are. It just seems surprising."

I take that to mean that Trump wonders who the people ignorant of his existence are and where they could have been hiding. Of course, the response might have been Trump's attempt to poke a little fun at himself — although it has to be said that no New Yorker asked by a survey-taker to identify Donald Trump would be likely to say, "Oh, he's the one with the keen sense of self-irony."

I think it's more likely that Trump was serious. This, after all, is a man who paints his name in huge letters on just about anything that will stand still long enough to be bought. This is a man who insisted to the compilers of the *Forbes* list of the richest people in the country that he was worth $3.74 billion, even though their best efforts could turn up only a billion. This is a man who seems to believe that giving to charity is not a true blessing unless you call attention to it. This is a man who boasted so widely about how he was going to have the Gorbachevs to an intimate little dinner while they were in New York that the Russians finally had to issue a public statement that was the diplomatic equivalent of "What's this guy talking about, anyway?"

After ten or fifteen years of such behavior, it seems to me, Trump could be genuinely surprised to hear that there are any human beings within the city limits — even a paltry six percent — who don't recognize his name. I'm surprised myself. After I read about the *Observer*'s survey, I found myself wondering who those people could be. And once I started wondering, I started thinking about Trump wondering.

I can imagine him trying to fall asleep at night, unable to get it out of his mind that there are people in his very own city who don't recognize his name. He tries to look on the bright side: only six percent of the people in the largest city in the United States don't know who he is. Maybe the six percent is made up completely of people who are simply out of touch with normal New York life — the sort of people who sleep on dirty pieces of cardboard in some forgotten subway tunnel. Wait a minute! The largest city in the United States! There are seven million people in New York. That means that six percent of them would amount to 420,000 people. There can't be 420,000 people living in subway tunnels. If the real estate industry continues to reglitz the city at the present rate, maybe someday there will be 420,000 people living in subway tunnels, but not now. Also, the survey was conducted by phone, and the people in subway tunnels aren't listed. Trump has to face it: 420,000 mainstream New Yorkers have never heard of him.

What to do? He could just keep mouthing off. He could buy larger companies and costlier yachts. But none of that has reached these people before. And he can't afford to let this stand. After all, he's on record in *Time* magazine as saying, "I just keep pushing and pushing and pushing to get what I'm after."

Then, rereading the *Observer* article, he discovers that the survey was based on a sampling of only 478 people, meaning that only 29 people represent the 420,000 New Yorkers who never heard of him. He obtains the 29 names and sets about to win them over. He invites them to parties on his yacht. He offers to get their names in the gossip columns. One by one they decide they had heard of him after all. "Oh, yeah, sure, Donald Trump," they say as they ride in the back of the limousine toward the yacht. "Why didn't you say so?"

There is one holdout, a surly auto mechanic from Brooklyn. No matter how many times Trump says, "You know me — right?" the auto mechanic says, "I don't know you from Adam, mister, so don't do me any favors."

Trump keeps raising the ante. In desperation he finally says, "I'll give you half of my fortune. You'd get almost two billion dollars."

"Get serious," the mechanic says. "Your fortune is only a billion altogether."

Trump is crestfallen. Then, suddenly, he realizes how the mechanic knows about the billion: he must have read in *Forbes* about Trump's attempt to inflate the figures. The mechanic has heard of Donald Trump after all. Trump holds a press conference. "I've won again," he announces.

Choice of Words

February 27, 1989

I'VE FOLLOWED the commentary of my colleagues on the John Tower confirmation controversy pretty closely, trying to decide whether the flap over Tower will have any long-term effect on the political process. About all I can think of is that it's now clear that nobody much likes the word "womanizer." I don't much like the word "womanizer" myself. It sounds like something you do with a machine.

I prefer the word "skirt-chaser." It's an old-fashioned word, of course. A lot of women don't even wear skirts anymore. (Old-fashioned people deplore that; they think a skirt tends to "womanize" a woman.) The image that the word "skirt-chaser" conjures up for me is, in fact, old-fashioned: I see the swirl of a skirt as a secretary rounds the desk, easily eluding her boss — a puffing, red-faced man who is desperately but unsuccessfully trying to keep his dignity. To me, in other words, a skirt-chaser is not necessarily someone who's successful in the chase.

"Womanizer," on the other hand, sounds to me like somebody who's smooth enough to make a chase around his desk unnecessary. I don't know if that's a common interpretation of the word — on "This Week with David Brinkley," Senator Tower himself suggested that it's a hard word to define — but I know at least one other person who understands it that way, a friend of mine I'll call Sheldon. Although Sheldon is single and seems perfectly presentable to me, he's one of those men whose invitation to dinner and a show seems to remind any woman of how desperately she needs to stay home that night and clean out her closets. Sheldon seemed cheered by the discussion of Tower's womanizing. "If John Tower's a womanizer," he explained to me, "there's hope for us all."

I'm not at all sure, though, that everyone sees those words the way Sheldon and I see them. It may be that someone nominated for high office ought to be given his choice of words. Some senior and widely respected member of the Washington press corps could simply approach the nominee and say, in the most respectful sort of way, "Excuse me, sir, but if we find it necessary to repeat rumors and gossip concerning your personal life, would you prefer to be called a womanizer, a skirt-chaser, a lech, or a dirty old man?"

I hasten to say that I personally have no firsthand information that would lead me to conclude that any of those words can be fairly applied to Senator Tower. I was not one of the people who was interviewed about the senator by the FBI. If I had been interviewed, I would have reported having seen Senator Tower twice in my life, once in the restaurant of a luxury hotel in Dallas and once in the cocktail lounge of a luxury hotel in Washington. I can't say that either instance provided any evidence that the senator is a skirt-chaser or a boozer — a word I prefer, by the way, to the more genteel "someone who abuses alcohol," which always conjures up for me someone who, when he gets to feeling angry and frustrated, is likely to slap around a bottle of gin.

Both times I saw the senator, he was looking extremely natty. On neither occasion was he standing on the table or flipping pats of butter at passing waiters. In neither case did I recognize the people he was with; for all I know, they might have been the senior deacon of his church and the president of the Women's Missions Society. When I think back on what went through my mind as I observed the senator — I believe that's the sort of thing FBI agents ask you to do — I remember thinking on each occasion, "I wonder how much he paid for that suit?"

That means, I suppose, that my testimony to the FBI would have contributed only to the evidence that Senator Tower is a clotheshorse, or maybe a dandy. Now that I think of it, those two words have different connotations. "Dandy" is a sort of old-fashioned word. I think of a dandy wearing spats, one of which might have come loose during the chase around the desk.

But some people might prefer "dandy" to "clotheshorse." Maybe it would be a good idea to give the nominee a choice of those words as well. That's true of the words for boozer, too, of course. It might make sense to hand out a form. "Would you prefer to be called a boozer, a hard drinker, an alcohol abuser, or a lush?" might be the final question. Except for "Would you just as soon skip the whole thing?"

Embarrassment of Riches

April 10, 1989

WHEN NEWSPAPERS BEGAN trying to provide their readers with a way to grasp the size of Michael Milken's annual salary — this was after the government prosecutors who indicted the noted junk bondist revealed that he made $550 million in 1987 — I didn't think the comparisons with the national budgets of smallish countries really came across. It's easy enough to say that if Milken were a country he'd have been Mauritania plus Rwanda, but it's difficult for readers to imagine some guy in Los Angeles as two countries.

At least those comparisons weren't terribly embarrassing to the countries involved. It's safe to assume, after all, that people in Rwanda aren't following this story closely in American newspapers, so saying that a guy in Los Angeles takes in a lot more than the whole country is no skin off Rwanda's nose. (Yes, if a guy in Los Angeles can be two countries, a country can have a nose.)

I thought the most embarrassing comparison the papers came up with had to do with McDonald's. A number of news stories said that if Milken had been a corporation ranked by annual sales, he would have finished just behind McDonald's. The folks at McDonald's must have read those stories, and they must have been mortified.

It wouldn't have been so bad if the papers had compared Milken's salary to the annual sales of one of those stuck-together American corporations with names that sound like typing exercises — JKL UniBlob, or something like that. Nobody actually knows what a corporation like JKL UniBlob does. For all the average citizen knows, the folks at JKL UniBlob may not be trying very hard. In fact, for all the average citizen knows, there may not be any folks at JKL UniBlob.

But the McDonald's people scurry around, desperately trying to make a buck, before our very eyes. In most of their places you can see right into the kitchen. Everybody seems to be going flat out. Cooks are flipping burgers as fast as they can flip. The man who presides over the flow of food is madly stacking cheeseburgers while keeping one eye on the Big Mac supply and the other on the McNuggets. These guys are knocking themselves out. Guys in thousands of other McDonald's outlets all over the world are knocking themselves out.

Through all of this effort, they manage to sell literally billions of hamburgers. And there is Milken in California. One guy! He doesn't have to chase down teenagers who are in the sack when they're supposed to be flipping burgers for minimum wage. He doesn't have to hire battalions of marketing men to make up cutesy names for his products, like McJunk. Armed with nothing more than a telephone and a computer screen (and, according to the prosecutors, a few inside tips), he makes about as much money as this entire corporation.

Not only that: until Milken was collared, the McDonald's people didn't even realize that he was what they were going up against. They thought they were competing with Burger King, and they thought they were ahead. They didn't understand that you can compare hamburger chains with guys in California. Before this came up, they would have said that it's like comparing apples and oranges. Now they know that if the point is how much money you make — and what have we learned in the last ten years if we haven't learned that the point is how much money you make? — it's no problem at all to compare apples and oranges. You either make more money in apples or in oranges. Simple.

Which means that Orel Hershiser isn't doing very well — at least not compared with how Michael Milken was doing before the feds came to the door. Orel Hershiser must have thought he was doing pretty well when the Dodgers agreed to pay him $2,666,667 a year. Actually, the Dodgers must have thought they were doing pretty well, because their revenues are estimated at something over $50 million a year. They're not doing very well either, as it turns out, but at least that's nothing for them to be embarrassed about. After all, it's only a game.

The same can't be said for the mob. That is not a game. According to an article I read in the *New York Times*, the Gambino crime family takes in an estimated $500 million a year. That's $50 million less than Milken. Think of it! Here they have an entire organization running drugs and shaking down contractors and breaking people's legs and shooting their competitors — in other words, working just as hard as the McDonald's folks — and they can't make as much as one guy in California. Now that's embarrassing.

Book Deal

April 24, 1989

MY PUBLISHERS COULDN'T SEEM to understand that what I wanted for my new book was simply the same publishing arrangement Jim Wright had. "I'll just take the straight fifty-five percent royalty deal," I told them. "I loathe quibbling."

My publishers said they had never offered more than a fifteen percent royalty to an author. I knew how to handle that one. I pushed back my chair and turned to my high-powered literary agent, Robert (Slowly) Lescher. "Let's walk, Slowly," I said. In a hardball publishing negotiation, this is a sentence that has to be said just right. Otherwise, it sounds as if you're saying that you want to walk slowly — giving the people on the other side of the table the impression that you're getting a little creaky in the joints and may therefore be vulnerable.

Slowly put his hand on my arm. He turned to my publishers and told them that I was understandably upset at being offered a fifteen percent royalty after hearing that another author got a fifty-five percent royalty even though he was a first-time author and his book was just a bunch of recycled high school graduation speeches that had caused a lot of people in Watauga and Haslet to sigh and look at their wrist watches the first time around.

"We didn't offer fifteen percent," my publishers said. "We said that we'd never offered more than fifteen percent."

I pushed back my chair again. "C'mon, Slowly, we're history," I said.

Slowly put his hand on my arm — although this was quite a stretch, because every time I pushed back from the table I got farther away from him. "Wait a second," he said, speaking to me but enunciating clearly for the benefit of my publishers. "I know how you feel, and I don't blame you. And I'm not saying we should accept the fifteen percent. But I think we should do our best to discuss this rationally, no matter how other people behave."

Gradually I settled back in my seat. "O.K., Slowly," I said, "I'm willing to give it one more try."

This was all part of our negotiating strategy, of course. Slowly knew I wasn't actually ready to walk. For one thing, he happens to know that I'm getting a little creaky in the joints.

Slowly turned to my publishers, slowly. "We'll stay," he said. "For the time being."

My publishers nodded. Then they started talking about why it's difficult for a publishing house to give an author even a ten percent royalty, considering how much publishers have to spend on, say, advertising and promotion.

"Wait a minute!" I said. "I know better than that." I pushed my chair back, just enough to make Slowly reach out toward me. I told my publishers that they could simply do what Newt

Gingrich's publishers did — raise a hundred grand or so in advertising and promotion money from my supporters.

"Your supporters?" my publishers said. "Which supporters are those?"

I glanced over at Slowly. He didn't look as if he wanted to pursue that. Instead, he asked my publishers what kind of sales they were anticipating. He asked them politely. That was also a piece of strategy, you might say: he didn't want to encourage them to remind us that my previous book had sold like poisoned hotcakes.

They reminded us that my previous book had sold like poisoned hotcakes.

"Hold it right there!" I said, pushing back my chair just a tiny bit. I told my publishers that the problem with the marketing of the previous book was their failure to use bulk sales. Picking up the House Ethics Committee report, I pointed out some bulk sales that Jim Wright's publishers had managed to make — to the National Association of Realtors, for instance, and to Mid-Continent Oil and Gas Association and to the unfortunately named but presumably literary-minded Fertilizer Institute. "The trouble with you people," I said, "is that you persist in trying to sell books one at a time."

My publishers said they didn't think the Mid-Continent Oil and Gas Association would be terribly interested in my new book. Then they asked if I had thought about trying to spice up my first chapter a bit with some old high school graduation speeches.

"C'mon, Slowly, let's vacate the premises," I said. I would have pushed my chair back, but I was almost up against the wall as it was. I was going to say we'd try Wright's publishers, but I couldn't think of the name; what kept coming to mind was the Pork Barrel Press.

Slowly managed to put his hand on my arm, although the stretch nearly caused him to fall out of his chair. "O.K.," he said to my publishers. "We accept the fifteen percent, but not a penny less."

Reading Deal

May 1, 1989

GAYFRYD STEINBERG, who is sometimes called the Queen of the New Society, has come forward to say that "rich people do read too." We all have a lot to learn about the rich.

Mrs. Steinberg made her point while complaining to James A. Revson, who covers the ball-gown set in New York for *Newsday*, that people persist in seeing something frivolous about her association with PEN, a good-works organization of poets, playwrights, essayists, editors, and novelists. According to Revson, Mrs. Steinberg helped transform PEN from "a rather dowdy, low-profile literary association" to something of passable glamour — a stop on the gala benefit circuit that can compete in glitz with some of this country's best-known dread diseases.

I happen to have had some experience with PEN in the pre-Steinberg era — they'll sneak a reporter in under the "essayist" category now and then if he promises to keep his little finger extended while drinking tea — and I can testify that Revson has that "dowdy" business dead right. (I can also testify that reporters never drink tea, but that's another story.) I remember noticing any number of frayed collars, a couple of them on my own shirts.

Enter Gayfryd Steinberg. In no time flat, PEN was holding an annual big-ticket black-tie benefit that brought together rich people and writers. The result was that PEN took in a lot of money for its good works, writers (some of them looking a bit dowdy, if you must know) got a free meal, rich ladies had another opportunity to wear their designer dresses, and everybody was happy — particularly the dress designers, who already had reason to be the jolliest folks in Manhattan.

And Mrs. Steinberg's reward? Sneers. Insinuations that she just wanted to get her picture in the paper hobnobbing with Norman Mailer so she could compete with the rich ladies whose charitable activities got them in the paper hobnobbing with Baryshnikov or Luciano Pavarotti. Implications that rich people don't read. As my Aunt Rosie in Kansas City used to say, "You do for people and you do for people, and where does it get you?"

The Steinbergs definitely have what people back in Kansas City tend to call "a bunch of money" — according to Revson, their apartment has thirty-four rooms and a staff of fifteen — but Mrs. S. says that money is no deterrent to reading. In fact, it seems to help. What she told Revson about their method of encouraging their children to read is this: "I have a reading list with dollar amounts." One kid recently got thirty dollars for reading *Shogun*, she said, and another kid made a quick twenty for knocking off *Of Mice and Men* by John Steinbeck.

That's all we know about the cash-for-reading scheme. Revson, that sly devil, told us that much and no more. We don't even know whether a high price tag means that a book is considered particularly worthwhile or particularly hard to get through. Or could it be that pricing is based simply on heft?

After all, I know some dowdy writers who would probably pay their kids not to read *Shogun.* On the other hand, *Of Mice and Men* is pretty short. Was it a five-dollar job before Steinbeck's Nobel Prize was factored in? Was *Shogun* considered labor-intensive? We don't know.

We're not told which of the fifteen servants at the Steinbergs' digs is in charge of pricing books. Is it possible that someone in the kitchen responsible for checking in supplies simply weighs the novels with the lamb chops? Most frustrating of all, we don't know the price tags on books written by the famous writers Mrs. S. has had her picture in the paper hobnobbing with. Have you no mercy, Revson?

We're left to imagine the confrontation between one of the Steinbergs' boys and Norman Mailer, the renowned novelist who has on occasion had his picture in the paper for brawling, as Mailer wanders through the apartment trying to figure out which of the thirty-four doors leads to the gents'.

"I just got a hundred and a quarter for reading *The Executioner's Song,*" the boy says, "and I want you to know I feel like I earned every penny of it."

"If you think I'm above decking a twelve-year-old, think again, kid," Mailer says as he starts to exit into a closet he has mistaken for the third drawing room.

Mailer's old rival, Gore Vidal, wanders by — although he's known as a worldly man, he's also lost — and says, "The other lad tells me that Gayfryd has that war novel of yours on discount special this week, Norman."

Mailer is furious. He cancels Mrs. Steinberg's hobnobbing privileges. PEN finds another rich lady to preside over its benefit. Mrs. Steinberg is unconcerned. She stays home that evening with a good book.

Pardon My French

May 22, 1989

ACCORDING TO THE NEWSPAPERS, people in France are worried that the French language may be losing out to English. I'm not worried about that at all. As it happens, I don't speak the French language. So far as I'm concerned, the faster the French language loses out to English the better. It doesn't even have to be very good English that French loses out to. I'd be happy to get in a Paris taxi and have the driver say to me, "To where are we be taking thou, sir?"

I would tell him to take me to the Pasteur Institute, which recently horrified even the President of France by changing the names of its scientific journals from French to English. Once I got there, I would say, in the manner of a British headmaster congratulating the winning rugby team, "Good on you, Pasteur Institute! Good on you!" Then I would give everyone at the Pasteur Institute a high five — what used to be called an *haute cinq* over there before the French language started losing out to English.

Then I would get back in my cab and go to the nearest bar, where I would say, in my best English, "Gimme a beer, Mac, and step on it." When the bartender answered, in English, I would refrain from criticizing his accent, despite all the times that French taxi drivers pretended not to understand my directions in the days when the French still spoke French. I'm above that sort of thing, although just barely.

Understand my directions? Yes, I'll admit it: I speak a little French. Not verbs. I've stated publicly that I gave up verbs in French a long time ago. I used to know verbs. In fact, I knew some pretty complicated verbs — what I believe the French intellectuals call Sunday-go-to-meeting verbs. For instance, if I wanted to know where the beach was, which I often did, I could say *"Où se trouve la plage?"* — which, literally translated, is "Where does it find itself the beach?" But that seemed silly to me. A beach knows where it is.

I retreated to the simpler verbs, but I found that doing even simple verbs was time-consuming. People would say, "What'd you do on your vacation in Paris?" and I'd say, "Well, I spent an awful lot of time trying to remember the conditional tense. Then we went to a couple of museums, and then I put in a day or so trying to get myself straight on the difference between the infinitive and the gerund."

If things keep moving our way, though, I won't even need any nouns. The head of the Pasteur Institute said that the institute simply had to face up to the fact that the international language of science is now English. He said that in 1988 the institute received 249 manuscripts, half of them from French-speaking countries, and only six percent were written in French. Good. I think if we really work on it, we might be able to get that down to about two percent.

I suppose you could argue even then that an absence of French content is no argument for changing the name of a scholarly journal. Think of all the restaurants in the United States that have French names even though the only thing French about them is the Kraft's French dressing they use at the salad bar. I suppose you could argue that, but I'm not about to. I say, in English, "Stick to your guns, Pasteur Institute."

That phrase itself, by the way, is an example of how much better everything is going to be when the French language finally loses out completely to English. In the French translation, it would mean people literally sticking to their guns — a bunch of people standing there with no one left to shoot but still unable to remove their hands from their guns. Getting rid of that sort of awkward and embarrassing image is going to be a big relief to the French, once they get used to it.

The same people who are so outraged by the decision of the Pasteur Institute are also outraged by the increasing presence of what's called Franglais, English words like *drugstore* and *fastefoude* that have crept into the French language. I don't find Franglais such an outrage. I think of it as a nice transition step toward all-out English. Also, since the increase in Franglais I have just about tripled my French vocabulary. If I cared to, I could say, *"Où se trouve le fastefoude?"* I don't care to.

When I arrive at the fast-food joint, I can order easily, since all the hamburgers in French fast-food joints already have English names. Then I can linger at a table, in the way French intellectuals have traditionally lingered at tables in the cafés to read their intellectual journals or scholarly quarterlies or political manifestos. What I'd read would be one of the journals of the Pasteur Institute.

Real Jeans

May 29, 1989

THE NEWEST THING in blue jeans is the ragamuffin look. That means wearing jeans with holes in them. Just about everyone in my high school wore jeans with holes in them now and then, of course, but that had nothing to do with the ragamuffin look. In fact, if you had congratulated one of the guys in my high school on the stylishness of his bold new ragamuffin look, he might have asked you if you were looking for a knuckle sandwich.

In high school, here's what I believed about blue jeans: anybody who wore anything but Levi or Lee blue jeans was a weenie, a nerd, a geek, a creep, and walked like a duck. In other words, I was a moderate on the subject. That was many years ago, of course, but I have never seen any reason to change my views.

When men started wearing designer jeans several years ago, I said to my wife, "Any man who wears designer blue jeans is a weenie, a nerd, a geek, a creep, and walks like a duck."

My wife argued for a little more flexibility. "That's an adolescent viewpoint," she said.

"Of course it's an adolescent viewpoint," I said. "It's the viewpoint I had when I was an adolescent. I have never seen any reason to change it."

Apparently, there are now people who make holes in their blue jeans for effect. In high school we wore blue jeans with holes because if we hadn't we could not have gotten our money's worth. Blue denim becomes more comfortable as it's worn and washed, but only six wearings after a pair of blue jeans achieves comfort perfection, holes begin to appear. It's a sort of formula — the only formula I remember from high school, as it happens.

This formula was proven in an experiment conducted at Southwest High School in Kansas City, Missouri, involving many pairs of blue jeans. I was present during the course of that experiment, and I can vouch for the soundness of the methodology. The experiment proved once and for all that using a pair of blue jeans is less like using a suit or a topcoat than it is like grilling a steak: at one point you have it just right. Six wearings later, it has holes.

There is a similar formula having to do with when shirts begin to fray and when they are absolutely comfortable. In the case of shirts, though, they can last in a comfortable state for something like eight months before they completely fall apart, usually at the elbows. This, I'll admit, is eight months during which you are likely to hear a lot from your wife about the condition of your shirt, but it is otherwise a blissful eight months.

I don't think it's at all surprising that I haven't changed my views on blue jeans — or on frayed shirts, for that matter — since high school. What is remarkable, though, is that the blue jeans themselves haven't changed. There are still precisely six wearings in them between the time they reach a state of comfort perfection and the time they start developing holes.

I know what the cynics are going to say: "Aha! Built-in obsolescence! All this talk about miracle fabrics and these sharks can't find it in their hearts to build in an extra perfect-comfort wearing or two before the holes begin to show up."

I wouldn't agree with that sort of thinking. Sure, there have been miracle fabrics developed since I was in high school, but nobody with any sense would put them into a pair of blue jeans. Once some of those things got into a pair of blue jeans it wouldn't be a real pair of blue jeans. As far as I'm concerned, anybody who wore blue jeans with miracle fibers in them would be someone who's a weenie, a nerd, a geek, a creep, and walks like a duck.

Naturally, I wore blue jeans with holes in them myself when I was in high school. Naturally, I still do. There is nothing whatsoever concerning blue jeans that I have changed my opinion about in any way since high school. This never presented a problem before. But now we have the ragamuffin look. The other night, while my wife and I were walking down the street in our own neighborhood, she gave my blue jeans — my blissfully comfortable blue jeans — one of her inspector-general perusals and said, "Are you trying to make a fashion statement?"

This is a troubling thing to say to someone who went to my high school. Do I want to risk being taken for someone who is striving for the ragamuffin look? I'm now considering placing on my blue jeans a small sign that says HOLES STRICTLY AUTHENTIC. But would anybody from my high school consider blue jeans that had a sign on them real blue jeans?

Chance of Showers

June 19, 1989

I'VE HESITATED TO REVEAL exactly why it began raining in New York one day this spring and was still raining six or eight weeks later. I've hesitated because telling the story makes it sound a little bit like I'm saying, "I told you so." But, I finally decided, so what? After all, I did tell them so. Also, I feel I must get this story out while I can. As the theologians tell us, no one of us is permitted to know his allotted span on this earth, and if it doesn't stop raining I could perish anytime from jungle rot or mold.

So here's the story. It all started with a drought. New York didn't have much ice or snow this winter, although, as far as I can tell, that had no effect on the normal winter crop of potholes. What it did mean was that the reservoirs were low, down to about half of what they were the previous year. Oddly enough, that's pretty much the way most people who live in New York feel after getting through any winter — down to about half of what they were the previous year. That's O.K. for people, but apparently it won't do for reservoirs. The experts said that the city was in danger of running out of water.

I need hardly tell you that there were a lot of ideas for conserving water. And I need hardly tell you that a lot of the ideas were pretty silly — what New Yorkers call cockamamie. Some of the flashier advertising guys, for instance, said they were trying to get everyone in the industry to sign a pledge promising to order martinis straight up instead of on the rocks until we got this thing behind us.

I hesitate even to bring up the preservation plan that called for people to shower together. It's embarrassing. I should say, just for the record, that people who tried to obliterate that scheme with ridicule misrepresented what it called for. For instance, even the most extreme proponent never suggested that the entire population be paired off by computer for shower-sharing. It was always assumed that you'd get in there with someone you knew pretty well.

Still, it was a dumb plan. As critics pointed out right away, doubling up on showers could actually result in more rather than less water being used. A single person in the shower is likely just to soap himself up and rinse off and sing maybe one chorus of "You'll Never Walk Alone" and get out. If you put two people in a shower together, they'll get to talking, probably about the drought, and the water is running all the time. This is particularly true if they've just had a couple of martinis straight up.

Most of the other conservation plans were just as wacky. They were summed up by someone as "Perrier-on-the-flowers schemes." Even if they hadn't been wacky, the water they conserved wouldn't have been enough to end the emergency. In addition to saving water, New York simply had to find more water — which is why, according to the word that was starting to get out sometime in May, the mayor was going to ask everyone to hope and pray for rain.

I warned against this approach from the moment I was told about it by a friend of mine I'll call Marvin, who's close to the mayor. "It's just too dangerous," I said. "There's no way to tell what will happen if he has seven million people hoping and praying for the same thing at the same time."

"The mayor figures that people in New York are so contrary that if you ask them to hope and pray, ninety percent of them won't hope and pray," Marvin said. "He figures that a lot of the rest of them will hope and pray for the opposite of what you asked them to hope and pray for, just as a matter of principle."

"It's not worth taking a chance," I said. "Tell him if he wants to ask people to hope and pray for rain, let him start by asking just the people on Staten Island. Then if we get some sprinkles, he can go on to the Bronx."

"The mayor doesn't like to do things in a small way," Marvin told me.

Fine. So the mayor asked everybody to hope and pray for rain, and now living in New York is like living in Cameroon. The reservoirs have reservoirs. You can swim in the potholes. When the mayor walks around City Hall, he makes a squishy sound. A lot of New Yorkers must be hoping and praying that this ends soon, but I hope they don't do so all at once. I don't want another drought.

Prom Night

July 13, 1989

AS FAR AS I'M CONCERNED, the newspapers tell us a lot too much about the dispute that Warner Communications and Paramount have carried on over Time Inc. while telling us far too little about the dispute Tomontra Mangrum and Marlon Shadd have carried on over the prom at Palm Beach Lakes High School. I'm always reluctant to criticize my brethren in the press, but that's how I feel.

The merger argument involving Paramount and Warner and Time is obviously just the same old story with different players. Ever since American corporate executives realized that there was less money to be made for themselves in minding the store than in buying or selling the store, takeover battles have amounted to a lot of repetitious tap-dancing in front of the curtain while the stage is being set for the grand finale — a lavish production number in which all production is done by the Japanese.

Yet thousands of trees were cut down to tell us every detail of this corporate drama. And how much space did the dispute between Tomontra Mangrum and Marlon Shadd get? The only item I could find back in May, when the story first hit the papers, was an Associated Press dispatch exactly two and a half inches long. It said that Tomontra Mangrum, who is fifteen, was suing Marlon Shadd, who is seventeen — the complaint being that she spent $50 on doing herself up for the high school prom he was supposed to take her to, and then he didn't show up. It quoted Marlon as saying that he had fractured his ankle and also that he had to go out of town that night.

All sorts of questions were left unanswered. First off, what kind of cad is this Marlon Shadd? Did he really expect anybody to fall for that business about being both incapacitated and out of town? Is Palm Beach Lakes High School the sort of place where a student can say "The dog ate my homework" and get away with it?

Somehow, we get a full curriculum vitae of every Time Inc. executive important enough to get a tiny cut of the sweetheart merger deal they finagled for themselves, but we're not even told how long Marlon Shadd and Tomontra Mangrum had known each other. Were Tomontra and Marlon, as the gossip columnists used to say, an item? Or was this to be their first date? Was this one of those rickety arrangements cooked up by the class movers and shakers to make sure that everyone had a date for the prom? Should the class movers and shakers be sued?

Or maybe something had happened between Tomontra and Marlon. Maybe Tomontra, joking around one day in the high school cafeteria, said something in fun about, say, Marlon's haircut that deeply wounded him — hurt him worse than a fractured ankle. Maybe I had been too quick to judge the boy as a cad. Maybe he was only a bounder. That worried me.

Here's another thing that worried me: how the guys I went

to high school with were interpreting this story. After all, they had no more information than I did, and, like most people, they still think about high school matters the way they thought about high school matters when they were in high school. Knowing that, I knew they assumed that Marlon must have been reluctant about taking Tomontra to the prom in the first place and then must have bolted when a better opportunity came along. They had not seen a photograph of Tomontra, of course, but they took it for granted that Tomontra was the sort of girl who's described by the people trying to get her a prom date as someone with a good personality.

Thinking about the way my high school friends were thinking about Tomontra made me madder than ever at Marlon. I decided Marlon was at least a cad and maybe a scoundrel.

Then, just when I thought we were going to hear no more about Tomontra and Marlon, I saw a tiny item in the newspaper — only the caption on a picture, really — saying that Marlon had given Tomontra a check for $81.28 to cover the damages. It didn't say why she got $31.28 more than her expenses. Pain and suffering? Whiplash? This we don't know. We know about every wretched penny of the Time Inc. caper, but this we don't know.

What we do know now is what Tomontra looks like, because the picture was of her holding the check. Guess what? She's a knockout. Marlon would have been proud to walk into the prom with her on his arm. The picture made me change my whole view of Marlon. Maybe he panicked. It must have made my high school friends change their whole view of Tomontra. I hope so.

Packing Greatness

July 17, 1989

I PACKED THE CAR for the trip to the summer cabin. I was magnificent. As usual, some of the neighbors gathered around to watch. They were quiet except for occasional polite applause, like an old-fashioned tennis crowd. When I turned the food processor on its side and slid it neatly into the hole left between a carton of books and a sack of groceries, for instance, they clapped. An ace!

Packing a car is my principal talent. It's a talent I get to demonstrate just twice a year, on the way to the cabin and on the way back. Actually, you couldn't really say that I demonstrate it on the way back, because there's no crowd watching. The summer cabin is not the sort of place where people live close enough to drift over if they see some excitement on the block.

I don't mind. I've read interviews with tournament tennis players who say that they'd play the way they do whether there was anybody in the stands or not, just for the satisfaction of doing something as well as it can be done. I agree with that. Still, I wouldn't mind a crowd at the end of the summer. Also, it seems a pity that people quite near the summer cabin are missing a demonstration of world-class skill simply because they don't happen to know that it's going on. My wife says that putting a notice in the county weekly would be inappropriate. It was just an idea.

She also thinks that building a small grandstand overlooking where I pack in the city would be inappropriate. Fine. I was never serious about that. As it happens, the people I spoke to at City Hall said that there would almost certainly be problems obtaining a zoning variance anyway.

Still, what I was thinking as I drove to the cabin this year in my brilliantly packed car was that it does seem a waste to make such little use of a serious gift. As I was musing on that, we passed a station wagon that, I couldn't help but notice, was miserably packed. I saw any number of holes that could have been filled by an expert packer. The result was that part of what should have been in the back of the station wagon had spilled onto the seats. Half of the back seat was taken up by what looked like a stereo system balanced on an ice cream maker; that meant that two children were squished into the other half. The woman in the passenger seat — presumably the children's mother — had a birdcage on her lap.

I could just imagine the damage poor packing had caused this family. I had managed a quick glance at the children as we passed the station wagon, and they seemed to be glowering at each other. They had undoubtedly been arguing over who could sit next to the only window available. The bitterness between them might last for years, or maybe a lifetime. The mother also looked unhappy. I could imagine what she was thinking: "Was this the sort of marriage I bargained for — a marriage with a birdcage on my lap?" The husband, his very manhood threatened by his car-packing failure, is babbling meaningless alibis: "The sun was sort of in my eyes. The ball hit a pebble. I can't understand this. This has never happened to me before."

I realized that I could have helped that family. At the same moment, I realized that there was a living to be made as a packing consultant. People hire consultants for everything these days — consultants to organize their kitchens and help plan their weddings and decide on the colors of their clothing. How much more useful to hire a consultant for packing the car!

I could see the station-wagon family packing the car for next summer's trip. They have decided to hire a car-packing consultant. Me. Discreetly, I have rearranged a box of books and opened a hole in which Mr. Station Wagon has placed the pastamaker that fell on his older child the previous summer.

"Brilliant!" he says.

"That's what we're here for," I say.

The children are bouncing around in the entire back seat, having just signed a pact to share their toys forever. Mrs. Station Wagon looks at her husband adoringly and says, "How shrewd of you to hire a car-packing consultant, Mr. Station Wagon."

Naturally, he is very grateful to me. "I'd love to put up a small grandstand next to the driveway so people can see you in action," he says.

"I think there might be a problem with the zoning variance," I say.

"Let me handle that," Mr. Station Wagon says.

"Well," I say. "If you insist."

Garbage Greatness

July 31, 1989

I HEARD ON THE RADIO about this family of four near Vancouver, British Columbia, that produced only three bags of garbage a year. I know that the people who put that story on the radio meant well, but to tell you the truth, it kind of ruined my week.

I can't remember the name of the family that produced only three bags of garbage a year. I'll call them the Retentives. The interview was actually with Mrs. Retentive, who chattered on cheerfully about separating newsprint from brown paper for the recyclers and asking the counterman to leave off the Styrofoam containers when she and the kids — little Dawn and Scott Retentive — dropped by a fast-food joint to pick up some takeout burgers. You had to admire the Retentives, and you particularly had to admire Mrs. Retentive, who sounded as if she'd stick to her guns even if the counterman responded to her request by saying, "C'mon lady! No pickles, O.K. But no Styrofoam! Gimme a break, willya?"

Also, it was a startling fact — that once you subtract what is collected for recycling or put in the compost heap for the garden or, for all I know, shipped to relatives as a holiday greeting, an entire family leaves a bag of garbage out there on the curb for the garbageman only three times a year. The neighbors probably gather around on those days and say things like, "Wow! Four months and twenty-two days since the last one!"

This story was on the Canadian Broadcasting Corporation; living in Canada in the summer, I have grown accustomed to hearing startling facts on the CBC. The same week I heard about the Retentives, for instance, I heard on the CBC that some varieties of whales are able to communicate at distances of several hundred miles. Hearing a startling fact on the CBC gets you thinking, and I appreciate that. For instance, the fact about a whale's being able to communicate with another whale several hundred miles away made me wonder about what he might be saying ("Can you still hear me?").

So at first I treated this story about Mr. and Mrs. Retentive and their two children as a startling fact. "Imagine that!" I said to my wife, which is the same thing I said to my wife when I learned how far a whale can communicate with another whale. She nodded and mumbled something like "Amazing" or maybe "Three bags is not a whole lot of bags."

We drove for a while — we were listening to the CBC in the car — while the reporter explained exactly how the Retentives managed to get down to three bags full. Mrs. Retentive talked a little more about how she avoided anything in the supermarket that came with the sort of wrapping or packaging that was going to have to end up in the unrecyclable, uncompostable garbage.

My wife was silent for quite a while. Then finally she said, "I hate Mrs. Retentive."

"Oh, you don't hate her," I said. "Because I know that you're concerned with the environment and sympathetic to any effort to deal with the solid waste problem. I mean, you may not get terribly excited when the subject of solid waste management comes up, but you certainly share Mrs. Retentive's goals. So you don't really hate her. You probably think that she went a bit too far with what was essentially a good idea, or something like that, but you don't hate her."

My wife was silent again for a while. Then she said, "No, I hate her. I hate Mrs. Retentive."

I didn't say anything for a while. We drove another ten miles or so, all the time listening to the story of how the Retentives trained little Dawn and Scott to recycle. Then I said, "I hate Mrs. Retentive, too."

After another few miles, my wife said, "Mrs. Retentive is undoubtedly a responsible person who's simply trying to set an example. We should all be grateful to her for reminding us how much more we can do to reduce waste. I feel guilty about hating her."

"Me too," I said. "I was just thinking about some cruel neighbor who starts waking up before dawn on garbage day and sneaking extra bags of garbage in front of the Retentives' house. I think I'm going to feel guilty about that all week."

I did. It ruined my week.

Error by Number

August 14, 1989

MY FRIEND JANE IS WORRIED that she may have a cockroach in her computer. She thinks she might have seen one crawl in through the slot where you put the floppy disks. Jane's got a problem on her hands.

I won't mention Jane's last name because she finds it a little embarrassing to have a cockroach in her computer. For one thing, it sounds sort of inappropriate — like taking your Honda in and telling the service manager you have reason to believe that it may have a guppy in the crankcase. Also, it is well known that the cockroach is not a solitary creature, and Jane doesn't want her mother to know of the possibility that her apartment is, to use a phrase mothers often employ in these circumstances, crawling with cockroaches.

She wasn't even telling her friends. I wouldn't have known about this at all if my own computer hadn't developed Disk Error 31. Here are the symptoms of Disk Error 31: occasionally, when you try to save what you've written, you erase what you've written instead, and in a sort of computer version of shouting "Boo!" the screen suddenly says "Disk Error 31." I realize that there are a lot of troubles in the world and I realize that a lot of people have problems that are much more serious than Disk Error 31, but I want to tell you that Disk Error 31 can sting.

I tried to find out what Disk Error 31 was. I figured that if someone took the trouble to number an error the number must refer to something, and if you knew what it referred to you might be able to figure out what to do about it. I figured there was a list somewhere explaining which error was which. One line would say, maybe, "Disk Error 29: Loose wiring" and the next line would say "Disk Error 30: A little joke from the manufacturer, in Seoul, Korea." The line after that would identify Disk Error 31.

It turns out that there isn't any list — or if there is, it's highly classified. It turns out that Disk Error 31 is like most computer problems: the software people tell you that it's your hardware and the hardware people tell you that it's your software. A third party may tell you that it's your software telling you something about your hardware, or vice versa. Nobody would admit knowing why this particular disk error was called Disk Error 31. Sometimes, just for variation, I would describe it as Disk Error 14. Same response.

After a while I quit trying to find out about it. Instead I just said it over and over again, the way some spacey people on the subway chant things, or I wrote poems about it. Here's a poem:

> What disk error is really not all that much fun?
> Disk Error 31.

Sometimes I imagined a scene in which one of the hardware people or software people is strapped in a chair and I am leaning against a desk in front of him. A twitchy-looking blond man with a scar is sitting in the corner. I am speaking in the correct tones sometimes used by a German line officer talking to a downed American pilot in a World War II movie. "I do hope you will agree to tell me what Disk Error 31 is," I say. "If not, Herr Mueller here has his methods."

Finally my friend James fixed my computer. James knows everything about computers — except, of course, what Disk Error 31 is. I often call him for computer advice, even though he spends most of his time in New Iberia, Louisiana, and I spend most of my time in New York. I have suggested that he think about getting himself an 800 number. In this case he made a house call. He fixed my computer by replacing everything inside it. One of the things he replaced contained Disk Error 31. We don't know which one.

Jane, who happened to be visiting at the same time, was so impressed that she asked James if he could answer "a rather embarrassing computer question." The question was what you do if you think you might have a cockroach in your system.

"Well," James said, "they've got these programs that are supposed to get all the bugs out, but I don't suppose they mean it that way." Then he didn't say anything. I think James was finally stumped.

Something suddenly occurred to me. I got everything James had taken out of my computer and put it all in the kitchen in the dark. Then, after a while, I turned the lights on to see if anything scurried out across the kitchen floor. It had occurred to me that the secret list might say "Disk Error 31: Cockroach in the system." But nothing scurried. Now we'll never know.

The Check's in the Mail

August 28, 1989

I SUPPOSE EVERYONE HAD a nice warm feeling back when President Ronald Reagan officially apologized to the Japanese-Americans who had been held in detention camps during the Second World War and signed a bill awarding them each $20,000 in compensation. According to an article I read recently in the *New York Times*, though, a year has now passed and the government still hasn't paid anybody anything. I found that surprising. I had assumed that once the President signs a bill authorizing payment, all you have to do is wait for the paperwork to get done and then checks start appearing in the mail — more or less the way your tax refund check appears, which is to say only a week or two after you needed it in the worst way.

Not so. First the money has to be appropriated. It would take $1.25 billion to pay everyone who has been found to be entitled to compensation. In this year's budget, which has not been passed yet, President Bush has asked Congress to include $20 million for compensation to illegally detained Japanese-Americans. At that rate, according to my calculations, the last people to receive their payments will get their checks about 104 years after their release from the detention camps. Well, they say the Japanese are a patient people — even if, as in this case, the Japanese in question happen to be Americans.

I suppose waiting 104 years to pay people what you've decided you owe them is an example of what diplomatic correspondents mean when they use that phrase "Washington has adopted a wait-and-see attitude." Actually, the whole system of not paying what you owe until it's appropriated is a general money-saver. I'm thinking of trying it with my dry-cleaning bill.

I suppose I would answer the first couple of statements from the dry cleaner with a polite note, something like, "After checking your statement and our receipts, our family has come to the conclusion that we definitely owe you the $87.25 you have billed us for dry cleaning. Congratulations. Please let us know if you'd like a ceremony. You will, of course, be notified when the money to pay this bill has been appropriated."

I think I could count on Mr. Warwick, who runs the dry-cleaning shop, to give me a call after that, and I'd have to explain how these things work — the budget process and the various compromises during committee hearings with my wife and, of course, the general policy of belt-tightening because of the deficit around our house that some economists, including the one who works as a loan officer at our bank, find ominous.

According to the article I read, belt-tightening is the reason that President Bush asked for only a tiny start on the money the government has decided we owe people for branding them as disloyal and imprisoning them behind barbed wire while their patriotic neighbors snapped up their property at knocked-down prices. I suppose the theory is that under belt-tightening you can't just pay out $1.25 billion all at once, since that is, according to the off-the-rack prices now being put on the Stealth bomber, the cost of almost three airplanes.

I would use the compensation situation as an example in explaining all of this to Warwick. "We're making a serious effort to cut back this year, Mr. Warwick," I'd tell him. "I'm hoping to get through a twenty-five-dollar appropriation for your bill this month, but the way my wife has been going over these things lately, I have to tell you that it could die in committee."

From dealing with Warwick over the years, I know what he would say to that: "Are you telling me that you're not cutting down on dry cleaning, but you're cutting down on paying for it?"

"Precisely," I'd say. "You're beginning to catch on."

Now that the press has brought this matter to the attention of the people in Washington, of course, it's possible that the compensation will be paid at a somewhat faster pace. Maybe the White House will figure out a way to speed up the payments just enough so that the last people paid will get their checks precisely a hundred years after they were allowed to leave the detention centers. The people in the White House always have a nice touch with centennials.

Until then, it might be good public relations to dress up the payments a bit, maybe with the sort of ceremony we were planning to have for Warwick until he started that nasty talk about lawyers. Or maybe they could just send everyone who's owed money a fancy, official-looking certificate with an eagle and a crest and a motto. Not "E Pluribus Unum." Maybe "It's the Thought That Counts."

Mark and Anne

September 4, 1989

"NO WONDER PRINCESS ANNE is getting rid of Captain Mark Phillips," my old Army buddy Charlie told me. "The guy never gets promoted."

"What are you talking about?" I said.

"Well, when they got married, he was Captain Mark Phillips, and now, sixteen years later, he's still Captain Mark Phillips. You'd think he'd be at least a major by now. He must be getting fitness reports that look like my junior high school report cards."

"I don't think he's actually in the Army anymore," I said.

"Of course, try to look at this marriage from his point of view," Charlie went on, as if I hadn't spoken. "He comes home from company headquarters after work. He's had a bad day. There was nobody to bomb —"

"He was never in the Air Force," I tried to interject. "I think he was a cavalry officer in the Dragoon Guards."

"— and his sergeant major has somehow forgotten how to stomp his feet before he does an about-face to leave the room, the way the English sergeant majors in the movies always do it. This sergeant major salutes and then does a sort of soft-shoe that just drives Captain Phillips up the wall. I mean, it's as if Phillips has been assigned some old vaudeville hoofer instead of a regular English sergeant major. And every time the sergeant major is reminded that his leave-the-room stomp has gotten kind of dainty, he says, 'Mustn't disturb the chaps below, sir,' even though the company headquarters is on the ground floor. So Captain Phillips gets home, and all he wants to do is take off his boots and have a drink and relax and have a nice dinner and try to forget about having this sergeant major who can't leave the room without doing 'Tiptoe Through the Tulips' on the way out. But there's his wife at the door saying, 'Guess what! Prudence Poofingham-Thistle's husband just got promoted to lieutenant colonel!' And she pronounces it 'lefftenant colonel,' in that snotty way, just to rub it in."

"Charlie, all English people pronounce it —"

"And she says, 'You used to say that Nigel Poofingham-Thistle had pretty much the same I.Q. as his saddle, and now just look where he is. I bet they give him plenty of places to bomb. I bet his sergeant major just about shatters the floorboards when he leaves the room.' "

"Look, Charlie, Mark Phillips is not in the Army. He's got some sort of business that has to do with horseback riding."

"So she says, 'You might as well just resign your little commission and go start that dude ranch in Surrey you're always talking about.' "

"Charlie," I said. "It's not a dude ranch. They don't have dude ranches in Surrey."

"And of course the dinner is burnt," Charlie goes on. "Because you know a princess is not really brought up to cook. In the palace she always had a courtier to open a can of soup for her anytime she wanted it. All she had to say was 'Cream of

Mushroom' or 'Spring Garden Vegetable' and this courtier had a pot on the stove and the can opener just whirling away —"

"I don't think courtiers —"

"And right through this burnt dinner, there's Anne nagging," Charlie said. "She's talking about how Portia Rimplesnitt's husband is a colonel, and even old Trevor Carstairs-Spod, who, everybody knows, still sleeps with his teddy bear, is a major. She's telling him that just about everybody in the country has a higher rank than captain. Look at Major Gray's Chutney! Look at Colonel Bogey's March!"

"Those are not real people," I said.

"And Captain Phillips has had about enough," Charlie went on. "All he wants to do is finish dinner and go off to shine his boots and spend some time on his hobby, which is rhyming 'dragoon' with words like 'croon' and 'moon' and 'June.' But try to see it from her point of view. I mean, she's absolutely right about what a piddling little rank captain is. Just take a look at some of the doormen they have over there in London — the ones who wear those dress uniforms and all of those decorations, like they're off to watch Emperor Hirohito surrender or something. Some of those doormen look like they're at least colonels. When I'm over there, I salute them half the time. Which is hard for them, because it's not easy to salute back when you're holding a door."

"Charlie," I almost shout. "Mark Phillips is not in the Army. If he were in the Army, the Queen could just promote him."

"Exactly my point," Charlie said. "And she could send him to Rangoon, or at least some place where there might be a monsoon. Instead, he's still a captain, in some place that doesn't even rhyme. No wonder Princess Anne is getting rid of him."

Computer Habitation

September 11, 1989

WELL, ALL I HAVE TO SAY is thanks a lot. I try to help out a friend, and how much cooperation do I get from you? Don't get me started. My friend Jane was absolutely dripping with anxiety over the possibility that a cockroach had climbed into her computer. So I said, "Don't worry, Jane, old thing. I'll just mention your problem in my column and a bunch of people will write in to offer suggestions, and one of those suggestions will surely prove to be your salvation."

Meanwhile, I tried to calm Jane down. I pointed out that she couldn't be certain that the cockroaches were in residence and that, even if they were, computer circuitry is known to be inedible. That did nothing for her, but I kept assuring her that it was only a matter of days before we heard from some reader who recalled a similar case from, say, a Manitoba computer newsletter of limited circulation but excellent reputation. Fat chance! Here's how many letters I got with suggestions for what to do about the possibility of computer cockroach habitation: None. Zero. A big zip.

In my innocence, I had taken it for granted that a solution

would be forthcoming. I had even allowed myself to believe that the solution would not be in the baffling language of those computer manuals whose instructions look like the formulas in the physics you didn't get to in high school because of a scheduling conflict with an absolutely vital shop class. I pictured it as the kind of solution you read in newspaper columns devoted to household tips ("Those mauve stripes that sometimes overtake a zucchini can be removed by an overnight soak in Epsom salts and a good beating").

The sort of letter I assumed we'd get would say, "If your friend believes that there may be cockroaches in her P.C., she should insert the disk of a computer game my teenage kids play called 'Rocket War Blood Splash.' Even a cockroach would have sense enough to flee."

"Not even one letter?" Jane asked me this week, looking more distraught than ever. (She had heard what she thought might be chewing noises from inside her computer, although she acknowledged that it could have been the machine digesting a letter she had written to her Aunt Hilda.)

There had been one letter, but I hesitated to mention it to Jane. It was from an old friend of mine named Tom Chaney, who, without offering any advice, said that Jane's problem reminded him of what had happened to his sister, Ann Matera. It seems that Ann — who's the city clerk of their hometown, the splendidly named Horse Cave, Kentucky — had so much trouble inserting a floppy disk into her computer that she consulted the local computer whiz, who also happens to be the mayor. He took Ann's computer apart and found a mouse.

I'm not talking about the sort of mouse you find as an accessory to a Macintosh. I'm talking about a mouse — a small, dead mouse. The mayor figured it was the same mouse that had short-circuited the wires of the city copying machine by a method that a high municipal official probably wouldn't think is appropriate to discuss in public.

I appreciate the fact that Tom comes from a part of Kentucky where a story about a cockroach is likely to inspire a story about a mouse, but the last thing I had intended by mentioning Jane's problem was to start a round of "Can You Top This?" I could just imagine storytellers back in Kentucky sitting on the bench in front of the courthouse swapping tales of computer critters. "Why, I remember the time ol' Lister Scroggins — the Scroggins with the droopy ear who lives back up at Bald Knob — had himself one of them Toshiba laptops," Earl says, "and one day it starts in a-thumpin', and old Lister looks inside and there's this two-foot garter snake lookin' him right in the eye."

"Why, that puts me in mind of Uncle Boots Hawkinson," Roy says. "When he was doing the books for the hog farm on that old IBM clone with a forty-megabyte hard drive of his, and out popped a squirrel with a walnut in its mouth."

I could see it happening — claims of prairie dogs deep inside Compaq 386S's and cocker spaniels leaping out of Epson Equity II's. What good was that going to do Jane? Then I thought of one way I could help her. I suggested that she write for advice to the mayor of Horse Cave, Kentucky.

Caring for the Rich

October 2, 1989

I'M RELIEVED that Prince Frederick von Anhalt has come along to explain the rationale behind the recent vote in the House of Representatives in favor of cutting the tax on capital gains. I've been trying to explain the theory of federal tax policy for years without much success. Who would have thought that all we needed to clear this up was a prince who lives in Beverly Hills?

A long time ago I tried to explain that one way to look at tax policy was as a statement of the government's values. For instance, the fact that you can deduct the interest on the mortgage of your house is a way of saying that there is a general public good in as many Americans as possible owning their own homes. The fact that you can deduct the interest payment on a second house reflects the feeling that a ski chalet in Colorado is also a nice thing. That's why a Wall Street investment banker who thinks he might like a mansion in East Hampton for weekends can count on coal miners and teachers and check-out clerks and postal carriers and the rest of his fellow taxpayers to help out with the financing.

At that time I offered one possible interpretation of the values reflected in what was then the policy of taxing capital gains at a lower rate than what was called, without irony, earned income: the government was trying to teach us that speculation is a more worthwhile way to make a living than work.

The cynics, of course, have never interpreted tax policy as a reflection of societal values. They think that the law on mortgage-interest deduction, for instance, has less to do with how much the average congressman values home ownership than with how much he values the construction industry. They like to point out that the 1986 tax reform law that was supposed to eliminate loopholes includes a list of exceptions, each written in a way that mentions no names but can apply to only one corporation or one rich campaign contributor — and that the list is so long that so far no human being has managed to read all the way through it. The cynics would say that a law lowering the tax on capital gains reflects nothing more than the simple fact that rich people have more influence in Congress than poor people.

But there is another way to look at tax policy: as a way of managing the economy. That is normally the rationale used to explain tax legislation that seems to favor the rich, and what it usually comes down to is a notion that is fairly simple to state: the less rich people have to pay in taxes, the better off the rest of us are.

It's simple to state but it's difficult to understand. It's like a parent saying, while spanking a child, "This is hurting me more than it's hurting you." In other words, it may or may not be true, but it's a concept hard to concentrate on if you're the one being whacked. That's why so many Americans had difficulty understanding what was meant by supply-side economics. Although I take it as a solemn duty to understand these matters so that I can explain them to my fellow citizens, it has taken me all this time to understand what was meant by supply-side economics myself: we have a limited supply of rich people, so we must always be on their side.

The traditional way of explaining tax breaks for the rich is some variation of the old smokestacks-mean-jobs argument, but that was obviously difficult in the case of arguing for a reduction in the tax on capital gains. The people who would benefit the most tend to make their living by fiddling with money rather than producing goods and services. There's no expanded assembly line involved, only an enhanced job market for limousine drivers.

That's why attempts to explain this in Congress got so murky. That's why some advocates resorted to arguing that a reduction in the capital gains tax would produce billions in tax revenues because all the rich people would run out to sell everything they owned to the Easter Bunny.

Enter Prince Frederick von Anhalt. While the jury was out in the cop-slapping case brought against his wife, Zsa Zsa Gabor, the noted thespian, the prince said, "The rich and famous should be treated differently. They bring the money into Beverly Hills." The prince, being a prince, was not afraid to state out loud the argument behind all that convoluted rhetoric in Congress. The difference in the two situations, of course, was in the response to the prince's analysis: in California, the jury wouldn't buy it.

Ma and Me

October 30, 1989

THERE'S JUST Ma and me now, and the telly. The younger kid went off to school. Friends ask us what it's like. It's like being, well, sort of, retired. Or maybe laid off. It's as if we had been working along pretty steadily at this factory and one day the factory moved to Arlington, Texas.

Feeling retired is probably why I brought up the possibility of getting a hobby. The hobby I had in mind was building birdhouses. I've never had a hobby. Also, I've never built anything before. Also, I'm not particularly interested in birds. Still, building birdhouses has the sound of a good hobby. "I could just set up a simple workbench in the basement, Ma, and put in a shelf to hold my tools," I told my wife. "Then I'd subscribe to some magazine like *The Birdhouser* so I could get tips and read the Letters to the Editor column and correspond with other people who were building birdhouses."

"I think you're just going through a stage," my wife said. "Also, if you're going to be an artisan, maybe you should warm up by changing a few lightbulbs. Also, there isn't any magazine called *The Birdhouser*."

That's probably right — the part about going through a stage. People talk about children going through stages, but we're all aware that grown-ups go through stages themselves. You know when you're going through a stage because friends start asking you what it's like. I remember that when we first got married, people asked me what being married was like.

"You talk about chairs a lot," I said.

That was true. I don't want to give the impression that I had never owned any chairs before I got married. I had a chair. But I couldn't remember ever having discussed chairs. I didn't have any policy on chairs. My entire experience with chairs was this: occasionally, I'd go over and sit down in one. When you get married, you have to talk about chairs. For all I know, it's in the wedding vows. It's definitely part of the stage.

Having children around is a long stage that is a lot different from just being married. You quit talking about chairs. Oddly enough, you don't actually need any more chairs, even though there are more people. Children don't sit down much. You can pretty much forget about chairs. But there are a lot of dishes to wash.

There aren't many dishes now. There's just Ma and me, of course, and the telly. We eat out more. We're not as emphatic about the necessity of sitting down for a regular family dinner to catch up with everyone's day. Actually, with both of us feeling sort of retired, there's not a whole lot to catch up on. The regular family dinner was pretty exciting there for a while. Having dinner with people in high school can be like getting the soaps in prime time. But if there are only two people, and if one of them can bring you up-to-date on his activities with one sentence ("I'm kind of thinking about building some birdhouses"), you don't actually need an entire dinner. And that means fewer dishes to wash.

I figure that my wife and I run the dishwasher about once a month. I'm thinking of adopting a policy of running it on the same day we pay the mortgage; it's a way to remember to do both of those things. I've never had any trouble remembering to pay the mortgage before, but I could get pretty distracted if I became heavily involved in birdhouse building.

Friends tell us that there is a lot about having children around that people in our stage must be happy to be finished with. I guess so. But all I can think of offhand is snowsuits.

"I sure don't miss snowsuits, Ma," I said to my wife one night at dinner. We were having what you might call a regular family meal. (She had rejected my suggestion that since we were eating chicken we didn't need to bother with plates.) "I didn't really enjoy buttoning all those buttons and zipping all those zippers, and then, ten minutes later, unbuttoning all those buttons and unzipping all those zippers."

"They've got Velcro on snowsuits now," my wife said.

"Oh," I said. "Well. I guess they would. Did I tell you I'm thinking about building some birdhouses?"

"I'm thinking about redecorating the downstairs room," my wife said.

"Good idea," I said. "We've got more room in the closet down there, now that we're rid of all those snowsuits."

"I'm thinking of a rocker over in the corner and maybe something overstuffed and good for reading next to the window."

"What are we talking about here, Ma?" I said.

"We're talking about chairs," my wife said. "And quit calling me Ma."

My Dentist

November 6, 1989

MY DENTIST — Sweeney Todd, D.D.S. — had his receptionist phone me to say that I should come in for an appointment. I figured Sweeney was having cash-flow problems again.

"What is it this time?" I asked the receptionist.

"He says that he was looking at your x-rays, and you need a crown in the lower left something or other," she said.

"I don't mean what is it with me," I said. "What is it with him? Did the kid's college tuition bill just come in? Wife redecorate the rumpus room? Would you mind just shouting back there and asking him how much he owes for what? I'd like to get myself prepared."

"I can't," the receptionist said. "He's in the Caribbean until next Tuesday."

"I was afraid of something like this," I said.

"Before he left he gave me a list of patients to call," she said. "He told me that he'll need you for an hour on the first appointment."

"An hour on the first appointment?" I said. "Sounds like

Jamaica. Or maybe Antigua. This is definitely no cheapie to the Bahamas. That time he went to the Bahamas he only needed me for a half-hour session with the hygienist. May I ask if he took the wife and kids?"

"And his in-laws," the receptionist said.

"Erghh," I said, with some feeling. "I think we're talking gold crown here. Maybe even root canal. Those in-laws of his live high off the hog."

I showed up for the hour appointment anyway. What was the alternative? I don't think I'm up to auto-dentistry. I can't imagine myself bellying up to the mirror, opening my mouth wide, and saying, "Is it just my imagination or does that bicuspid look a little shaky?"

I could switch dentists, of course, but I've become sort of used to old Sweeney. If you listen closely while he's working on your teeth — you have to listen closely because, being rather clumsy, he makes a lot of noise banging the instruments around — you can hear him mumbling about whatever expense in the Todd family it was that got you into the chair in the first place. After years of that, I suppose I'd feel something was missing if a dentist didn't accompany his drilling with a lot of talk about how much electricians charge for a simple rewiring job these days.

Besides, I don't know any other dentists. I don't admit that to Sweeney Todd, D.D.S., of course. In fact, I've been telling him for years that some friends of mine are always singing the praises of the dentist they all go to, a relatively recent arrival from Kyoto known to his grateful patients as Magic Fingers Yamamoto.

"They say he's got the touch of an angel," I said of Yamamoto as I settled into the chair and prepared myself for the assaults of a deeply tanned Sweeney Todd, D.D.S. I had to raise my voice a bit, since Sweeney, in his effort to recover a mirror he had dropped, had knocked the rest of his instruments onto the floor.

"Open wide, please," Sweeney said. He has never been affected in the slightest by talk of Magic Fingers Yamamoto.

"Also, Yamamoto belongs to some Buddhist sect that believes the exchange of large sums of money corrupts the soul," I continued. "For crowns and bridges, he does wonders using the same material used for the common paper clip. His fees, of course, are nominal. Basically, he seeks his rewards in inner fulfillment. He spits on money — or he would if he weren't so polite."

"Spit, please," Sweeney said.

Sweeney had stopped his banging around and was standing next to his instrument cabinet peering at some x-rays. "What do you see there, Sweeney?" I asked. "A new transmission for your BMW? A long weekend with the missus in the Adirondacks?"

Sweeney held the x-rays up to the window to get a better look. "Won't be able to get away for the next few weekends," Sweeney said. "We're doing an addition to the kitchen."

"You never cease to amaze me, Sweeney," I said. "I've seen those television commercials that show doctors seeing all sorts of little bitty doodads through the miracle of CAT scans — or not seeing them, really, because all of the patients in those commercials turn out to be O.K. — but you've got to be the only medical man who can look at an x-ray with the naked eye and see an addition to your kitchen. What's your secret?"

"I have a better x-ray machine," Sweeney said, knocking over the water glass as he turned toward me. "But it's expensive. Very expensive. Open wide, please."

Part of the Plan

December 4, 1989

I RAN INTO A FRIEND of mine who told me that everything that has been happening in Eastern Europe is part of a setup. He said that the Communists are faking it in order to lull us into a false sense of security. And what happens when we're safely lulled? Then, he said, whammo!

I've grown accustomed to hearing him say this sort of thing. Years ago, Russia and China appeared to have fallen into a geopolitical version of what the old gossip columnist Walter Winchell used to call the don't-invitums, a phrase Winchell reserved for people so angry that they couldn't be asked to the same party, but my friend told me that the Russians and the Chinese were faking it. This was when Russian soldiers and Chinese soldiers were occasionally trading pot shots along the border, and Mao and Khrushchev seemed to be trying to think of the nastiest things they could say about each other. Mao, for instance, said that Khrushchev was in a "revisionist quagmire."

I figured that one really got to Khrushchev. I could imagine Khrushchev just wincing when he read that "revisionist quagmire" line in the newspaper. I could see Khrushchev's beady little eyes misting over as he put down the paper and said something like, "That Mao really knows how to hurt a guy."

My friend — I'll call him Harvey — didn't see it that way at all. "Believe me," he said when I commented on the zingers old Mao was sending Khrushchev's way, "it's a setup."

"How can you tell?" I asked. "It seems to me when you're in an argument with somebody and you get so mad that you say he's in a revisionist quagmire, there's really no going back. You can try to make up, but every time the guy looks at you, for the rest of his life, he's going to remember that you accused him of standing knee-deep in all that ooze."

"It's all part of their plan," Harvey assured me. "Don't be taken in."

Harvey would describe himself as a fervent anti-Communist — he is always telling me how wicked the Communists are — but there is probably nobody in the world who has more faith in the limitless ingenuity of Communism's rulers. Harvey has always thought that just about everything is part of their plan.

"If these guys who run Russia are so smart," I've been saying to Harvey for years, "how come everyone has to stand in line for soap over there?"

"Because Communism is not only wicked but unworkable," Harvey would say.

"Well, good," I'd say. "Then we don't have to worry so much about it."

"That's what they want you to think when you read about the lines for soap," Harvey would say. "Don't be taken in by that. It's all part of their plan."

"You mean they want everyone to be dirty?" I'd say. "I don't see how that could serve their purposes."

"Just wait," Harvey said.

So I waited. So did the people in the soap line. I was a lot better off than they were, of course, because I could do my waiting inside. Sometimes I would think about those people standing in line in Russia. I would think about what they might say if they knew about Harvey's believing that the line they were standing in was all part of a plan. It might cheer them up. "Guess what," one of the people in line would say as he stamped his feet and clapped his hands together in an effort to keep warm. "The bozos who run this country are too dumb to make soap, and there's a guy in Pennsylvania who thinks that's very clever of them."

So I'm used to Harvey. Still, I have to say that I was surprised to hear him say that even the recent changes in Eastern Europe were all part of their plan.

"But the East German parliament voted to end the special role of the Communist Party," I reminded him. "There were nearly a million people in the square in Prague shouting for the Communist government to resign."

"They've always been good at getting out crowds," he said. "Did you notice all those people were chanting the same thing and holding the same flags? Staged. Believe me."

"And Poland?" I asked. "Where they had to give up power? Is that part of their plan?"

Harvey nodded.

"Harvey," I said. "Maybe all of this is part of their plan, but it's not a very good plan. Maybe they made the mistake of putting the guy who was in charge of soap distribution in charge of the plan."

Harvey considered that possibility for a while. Then he said, "That's what they want you to think. Don't be taken in."

Wrong, Wrong

December 18, 1989

A PLEASANT BY-PRODUCT of the recent events in Eastern Europe is the way they have demonstrated that nearly everyone who has written anything on the subject in the past twenty or thirty years has been dead wrong. For people like me — people who tend to respond to all authoritative pronouncements by muttering, "Tell it to your grandma, buddy!" — a thoroughly convincing demonstration of the experts' persistent lack of expertise is always a great comfort.

For years, commentators on the left have been informing us that it's a stale old Cold War delusion to believe that Eastern European governments were maintaining their control over a captive people only through their power to call in Russian tanks. Wrong.

The Reagan Administration's rationale for cozying up to right-wing dictators while battling the wicked Commies was Jeane Kirkpatrick's theory that a Communist government, being what she labeled totalitarian rather than authoritarian, could never surrender power to a democratic government. Wrong.

A year or so ago, there were any number of articles explaining that, perhaps because of the native industriousness of the German people, East Germany seemed to be one country where Communism actually worked. Wrong. Wrong. Wrong.

Just this last July, Martin Peretz, in the *New Republic*, wrote, "The cheer with which Western commentators greeted Mikhail Gorbachev's tease that the Berlin Wall might come down 'when the conditions that generated the need for it disappear' is another sign of how credulous we have become in receiving blandishments from Moscow." Wrong. Gloriously, almost creatively, and quite specifically wrong.

In other words, people who considered themselves authorities on world affairs simply didn't know what they were talking about. This is just one more indication that anytime you see someone on one of those Sunday morning television news programs speaking with great authority on any subject, you are probably safe in remarking, "I believe that fellow has his big toe stuck in his ear."

Some years ago, when assorted malcontents and wackos began to catch on to how simple and satisfying it was to hijack an airplane in this country, the government began to talk about the possibility of installing the airport security devices that are now a routine part of air travel. When this rather drastic move was being considered, any number of learned psychologists were quoted as saying that it would of course cause an increase rather than a decrease in hijackings, because the sort of person thinking about such a caper was the sort of person who would consider security devices a challenge to be overcome. Wrong again.

We should have known the psychologists were wrong, because of the use of the phrase "of course." Anytime an authority begins a sentence with "of course," he is almost certainly wrong. I realize that I occasionally begin sentences with "of course" myself. I am often wrong. The only thing I can say in my defense is that nobody has ever considered me an authority on anything.

Another indicator of how likely it is that the authority is wrong is the size of the group of people whose opinions he purports to know. When I worked as a junior employee of a news-magazine many years ago, I often heard the story of a lofty editor, a man untainted by experience as a reporter, who arrived in London late one night to begin a tour of the European bureaus and started a cable back to New York the next morning with the words "The people of England believe . . ." The possibility of being right varies in inverse proportion to the number of people being talked about. A traveler who reports the opinions of his taxi driver may be right, if predictable. A foreign-affairs specialist who tells us what "the workers of Poland" now want could be partly right, but only by coincidence. The authority who begins a sentence with "Everyone knows" is almost certainly wrong. Wrong. Wrong.

Four or five years ago, an entertaining book was published under the title *The Experts Speak: The Definitive Compendium of Authoritative Misinformation.* The authors, Christopher Cerf and Victor Navasky, gathered together 391 pages of confident statements about how Hitler would never come to power and why *Oklahoma!* had no chance of success on Broadway and how "truth will become the hallmark of the Nixon Administration."

Despite their claim to definitiveness, the authors may have only scratched the surface of wrongness. I suspect that if they organized a symposium of authorities in the field, those assembled could come up with hundreds of other quotations and any number of other theories on how to predict the likelihood of an authoritative pronouncement's being absolutely wrong. There would, I assume, be some people in the back rows who would respond to the theories by mumbling, or maybe even shouting, "Tell it to your grandma, buddy!" Right.

Donk, Donk

December 25, 1989

TELEVISION EXECUTIVES live in mortal fear that everyone who is watching their channel is about to flip the dial. When television executives are feeling particularly insecure — that is to say, all the time — they think they can actually hear that little *donk* sound that a remote-control device makes when it switches to the next channel. There they are in their flashy offices, supposedly listening to some nervous independent producer pitch a sitcom, and all they can hear is millions of remote control devices: *donk, donk, donk, donk.* No wonder television executives so often act like donks themselves.

When a television executive conjures up his vision of paradise — no small feat, considering the distraction of a constant donking chorus that sometimes makes the inside of his head sound like the construction site of a new dollhouse subdivision — what he sees is a lump of human flesh planted in front of a television set that is beaming the right channel all day. The lump of flesh never moves.

There are, in fact, many such lumps. According to a recent article in the *New York Times*, ABC's "World News Tonight" may owe its ratings lead in the New York area to the fact that Oprah Winfrey's show on the ABC local channel easily outdistances Donahue (NBC) and Geraldo Rivera (CBS) at four o'clock in the afternoon, and the lumps just sit there motionless for the next two or three hours.

The writer of the *Times* article, Walter Goodman, suggested that ABC might do even better if it had Oprah Winfrey as the anchor of "World News Tonight." If you have real confidence in the lump factor, though, ABC would do even better than that if it presented Oprah Winfrey doing the sunrise prayer every morning at six and then just coasted on through the day from there.

No television executive has the nerve to try such a scheme, so the effort to maintain the viewers as lumps still depends mainly on what old-timers would call the Sullivan Tease. On his variety show, Ed Sullivan would cut to the commercials by saying something like, "And now, after this announcement, stay with us for the Fabulous Fontinis and Their Trained Antelopes, Jo Stafford, and, right here on this stage, twelve thousand tap-dancing Peruvian dentists."

Sullivan was operating in the days before remote control. He didn't hear that *donk-donk-donk* sound inside his head; he heard only the tapping of twenty-four thousand Peruvian feet. These days the pressure is greater. The theme music at the end of the evening news is accompanied by a voice-over informing us of all the joyously inane goings-on we can expect to find in the evening's sitcoms if we lump it out. Between sitcoms, one of those local anchors with perfect teeth comes on to tell us what disaster we can look forward to hearing about in detail on the eleven o'clock news. If you stayed up late enough to watch the sign-off, I suspect you'd hear about the delightful morning prayer you have in store for you if only you resist the temptation to change channels in your sleep.

I occasionally find myself in front of the tube during the evening. I like to watch "thirtysomething," for instance, because it is full of what my daughter calls snags — sensitive new-age guys. When those guys act particularly sensitive, I like to yell old-timer insults at them, like "Panty-waist!" or "Cream-puff!" My wife says all that wasn't funny even the first time I did it, but I enjoy the simple pleasures.

So I'm used to seeing the people with perfect teeth come on just after a commercial break to encourage me toward lumplike behavior. The other night, one of the perfect-teeth people got on during three commercial breaks in a row to tell me what I'd hear if I stayed tuned for the eleven o'clock news — the details of a fire and a couple of wars and a few drug busts. Fine. But then he said that I'd also find out whether there was going to be a blizzard during the morning rush hour.

Get this: Perfect Teeth knew whether there was going to be a blizzard during rush hour or not, but he wasn't going to tell me unless I stayed up for the eleven o'clock news. This is carrying the Sullivan Tease to a new level. At first I was going to make an angry call to the network. Then I realized I had a simpler response at my disposal. *Donk.*

Noriega's Undies

January 1, 1990

AT THE RISK of being considered unpatriotic, I have to say that I was not thrilled by the spectacle of American soldiers making sport of the contents of Manuel Noriega's underwear drawer. If that sort of thing isn't against the Geneva Conventions, it ought to be.

The American military command in Panama issued a two-and-a-half-page statement on General Noriega's bad habits, written as a sort of prosecutor's brief to prove that Noriega is what the Army called "a truly evil man." Based partly on what was found in Noriega's headquarters, the report said that Noriega was the sort of fellow who snorted cocaine and kept a mistress and enjoyed pornography and practiced voodoo and owned a picture of Hitler and was "a conditioned drinker" and wore red underwear to ward off the evil eye.

I don't think I've ever run across anybody who had all of those habits at once, but I could match some sinner of my acquaintance with just about every one of them individually. If "conditioned drinker" is another way of saying that someone can hold his liquor, I have sometimes felt late in the evening that I don't know quite enough of those.

I even knew an old fellow in Kentucky who believed in the efficacy of red underwear in keeping bad luck at bay, and I have to say that it seemed to work pretty well for him. I don't think the evil eye got anywhere near him, although that might have been because of the garlic he chewed as a second line of defense. In fact, wearing red underwear seems to me to have some advantages over more common methods of courting good fortune — consulting astrologers, for instance. It's low-cost and it keeps you warm. As my friend from Kentucky might have said himself, "Don't knock it if you ain't tried it."

I wouldn't for a moment deny that even before our military started poking around in his bureaus it would have been easy to make a case for the proposition that General Noriega is "a truly evil man." I won't even dwell on the probability that somewhere in the world, some other truly evil man who has his heel on the people of some other country — some man who has never thumbed his nose at our President, maybe, or who is considered reliably anti-Communist, or who might just run a country that is too large to be conveniently invaded — is probably sitting down to dinner with an American ambassador tonight and exchanging amicable toasts.

But still. When a television newscaster said, with some enthusiasm, that our soldiers were blaring rock music toward the Vatican Embassy as a way of mocking Noriega's love of opera — maybe his only ennobling characteristic — I did not say, "That'll show that Puccini-lover!" Somehow the sight of an American infantry commander, General Maxwell Thurman, holding a briefing for combat correspondents to reveal the sinfulness of Noriega's domestic arrangements did not leave me grateful that a nasty hoodlum had been humbled before the world. It just conjured up in my mind the phrase that so many Americans have heard from a parent at one time or another during their childhood: "Don't get down on his level."

And was I also above making cracks about the possessions of Ferdinand and Imelda Marcos after their sleazy palace was exposed to the world? Wasn't I the joker who said it was difficult to believe that Mrs. Marcos was able to break in all of those shoes without the use of political prisoners?

Well, yes. What do I claim is different about this situation? Maybe I simply expect a four-star general in the Army of the United States to behave better than I do.

But maybe the difference is that the Marcos palace was opened for the world to see by Filipinos, just as Baby Doc's wondrous digs were trashed by Haitians and the ill-gotten luxuries of the Ceausescus will be poked through by Romanians. Considering everything that Noriega has done to Panamanians, General Maxwell Thurman did not seem perfectly cast as the avenging party.

Considering everything that Noriega has done to Panamanians, you might argue, it seems overfastidious to object to our side's ridiculing his choice of undies. I would say that considering everything Noriega has done to Panamanians — symbolized for many Americans by the pictures of his goons attacking the candidates he stole the election from — we didn't need to be told that he was the sort who kept girlie magazines and wore red underwear. We particularly didn't need to be told by the people who were supposedly there to bring him back to the United States for a fair trial.

The Smaller They Are

January 8, 1990

WHAT IS NOW WIDELY SPOKEN OF as George Bush's political triumph in Panama merely confirms a theory of presidential popularity I have been working on for some time: the best thing a President can do for his approval rating is to stage a very large invasion of a very small country.

Ronald Reagan taught us that in October of 1983. It wasn't so obvious then. For generations, after all, it had been part of our heritage that the American people, with their ingrained sense of fair play, always like to root for the underdog. Who would know that the way to impress them was to send the American Army to conquer Grenada, population eighty-seven thousand? Ronald Reagan knew it instinctively — displaying, as usual, the sort of uncanny ability when it came to gauging public opinion that Dustin Hoffman in *Rain Man* displayed when it came to counting matches.

I know what you're going to argue. You're going to argue that a President's popularity goes up not because of an invasion but because of what it accomplishes — protecting the American medical students who were studying in Grenada, for instance, or arresting a nefarious drug trafficker in Panama.

I'm afraid not. Nobody remembers for long what an invasion accomplished or why it was supposedly undertaken in the first place. Who now remembers that the announced reason for the Israeli invasion of Lebanon was the shooting of an Israeli diplomat in London? Among experts there is widespread agreement that Noriega's arrest will have no effect on the drug trade — except, perhaps, in its reminder that our government was willing to keep a known drug trafficker on its payroll for years. Are you arguing that the next time you show up in an emergency room and find out that you're going to be treated by a doctor who was trained in Grenada you're going to give special thanks to Ronald Reagan? Forget it. What endures in the public mind is that Grenada is a very small country and we conquered it with a very large invasion.

Grenada was apparently the only very small country Ronald Reagan could find that needed invading — although, to give credit where credit is due, not many people knew that Grenada needed invading before Reagan invaded it. He sent soldiers to no middle-size countries, unless you count Lebanon. Reagan never counted Lebanon. In fact, as soon as a bunch of the people he had sent over there got killed, he quit mentioning Lebanon and invaded Grenada. I wouldn't be surprised to read in one of these kiss-and-tell books about the Reagan Administration that the White House had maps of the world that didn't show Lebanon at all; in the place where Lebanon is on most maps, Michael Deaver would have drawn in a little smile face and written next to it, "Let's talk about how it's morning again in America."

Poor Jimmy Carter had the theory upside down when he

ordered the commando mission that was meant to rescue the American hostages held in Iran. What he did was to sponsor a very small invasion of a very large country. Carter apparently was still laboring under the impression that the lesson of Vietnam was that the United States should be wary about involving a large number of its troops in another country. Reagan somehow sensed the real lesson of Vietnam: if you're going to involve a large number of American troops, find a country a lot smaller than Vietnam to invade.

Bush learned the lesson from Reagan. He kept his eyes open for another very small country that needed invading. For all we know about Grenada these days, it might need invading again, but Bush, a man known for his prudence, obviously didn't want to see what would happen if a President staged a very large invasion of the very same very small country some other president had invaded. Panama is larger than Grenada, but it is still pretty small. It is, the way I figure it, almost exactly a hundredth the size of the United States. In other words, Panama being invaded by the United States is the equivalent of the United States being invaded by a country of twenty-four billion people. (Yes, we might still have an edge in military hardware, but think of what a country of twenty-four billion people could do with human wave attacks.)

Before everyone forgets why we invaded Panama and what we accomplished there, Bush should take credit for one more thing he managed to accomplish: he put to rest the fears of any Russians who thought that, no matter what we said, we could launch a first strike against their country. It's now obvious that at the rate we're going we wouldn't get to a country the size of Russia for another two or three centuries.

Dental Problems

January 15, 1990

APPARENTLY, A LOT OF DENTISTS are mad at me. They write letters claiming that I insulted their entire profession in a column I wrote about my own dentist, Sweeney Todd, D.D.S. It's all a misunderstanding, of course, as anyone who knows what a fair-minded and sweet-tempered person I am could tell them. I didn't mean to insult the entire profession of dentistry. I only meant to insult Sweeney Todd, D.D.S. Still, I am not comfortable with the thought that there may be dentists all over the country who bear me a grudge. What if I got a toothache in a strange town?

As it happens, my teeth don't travel well. There is a theory that they are badly affected by changes in time zones. They seem particularly vulnerable to horrific flare-ups in Europe — I can't count the number of times a strange dentist has peered into my mouth and exclaimed, "Caramba!" or "Quelle tragédie!" — but it's always possible that a counterclockwise time-zone crossing could bring me acropper in, say, Amarillo or Spokane.

I could see myself limping into the office of the nearest

strange-town dentist. (Yes, a toothache can cause me to limp. I don't know why. We're all put together a little bit differently.) The dental assistant has settled me into the chair and assured me that Dr. Rasputin will be with me momentarily. I am holding my jaw and moaning softly. In walks Dr. Rasputin. "Well, let's see what we have here," he says in a confident and reassuring tone as he picks up the chart. Then he reads my name. It takes a moment to register. It registers. "You!" he shouts. He strides toward the chair, picking up his drill on the way. "You!" he repeats. "Slanderer! Dentist-basher! Smart-aleck!" I can't reply. I have fainted.

As luck would have it, I was about to start some traveling just as the angry letters began arriving. The scene in Dr. Rasputin's office haunted me. My wife told me that I was overreacting. "Not every single dentist in the United States is out to get you," she said.

Somehow, I did not find that reassuring. I felt that I needed a plan. I decided that if I got a toothache while I was traveling in a strange town, I would go to the dentist under an assumed name — perhaps even a name that might bring out in the dentist feelings of respect rather than a desire for vengeance.

I could see myself limping into Dr. Rasputin's offices again. My limp has become a little worse. With one hand, I hold on to a chair for support; with the other hand, I hold my throbbing jaw. The receptionist, a palpably kind young woman, says that she will do her best to fit me in, despite Dr. Rasputin's busy schedule. She takes out a Patient's Data Form and inserts it into her typewriter. "Name, please," she says.

"Archbishop Desmond Tutu," I say.

She types that in. Then she asks me other pertinent questions to complete the form. Then she says, "Just have a seat, Archbishop Tutu. I'm sure it won't be long."

My wife told me that my plan would never work.

"Well, then, how about Vaclav Havel?" I asked. "Or maybe Lech Walesa."

My wife said that the sensible way to approach the problem was not to sneak around under an assumed name but to demonstrate to the angry dentists that the column did not actually insult the entire dental profession.

I could think of some arguments along that line. The offending column, after all, was quite specifically about Sweeney Todd, D.D.S., and the eerie correlation between his diagnoses and his cash-flow needs — what those of us who are his patients sometimes refer to as the old root-canal/kitchen-redecoration connection. I can't imagine why other dentists — including, I blush to admit, the president of the American Dental Association — would see it as a general attack on dentistry and a way of encouraging my fellow citizens to avoid needed dental work.

If I were the sort of respectable columnist who analyzed world affairs in a profound and responsible way — I know it's hard to imagine, but just for the sake of argument — I wouldn't take a letter attacking a scurrilous, dentist-bashing, smart-aleck columnist as an attack on me. When I have a toothache, I hurry to the dentist without worrying about whether or not I might be helping to pay for his BMW. I wouldn't suffer just to see Sweeney drive a clunker.

Also, I could point out, Sweeney Todd, D.D.S., actually liked the column. I'll admit I was hesitant about going in there after the complaints started. There was no way to hide; Sweeney knows very well that I'm not Archbishop Desmond Tutu. But he welcomed me cheerfully. He told me that the column had brought him more patients at a time when he was particularly eager to be of service. Then he told me what a house in Nantucket can cost these days. Then he said, "Open wide."

Cover Boy

January 22, 1990

IN ALL THE EXCITEMENT over the changes in Eastern Europe, I didn't pay much attention to commentators who warned that ending the grim stability of the Cold War could make the world dangerously unpredictable. Then Mikhail Gorbachev appeared on the cover of *Vanity Fair*. That one stopped me. Before all this turmoil, you could count on the cover of *Vanity Fair* for straight celebrity flash: Daryl Hannah or Kevin Costner or Bruce Willis or Jessica Lange or, it almost goes without saying, Michael Jackson. It's not that *Vanity Fair* had never had a political figure on the cover except for Princess Di; Ronald and Nancy Reagan were on the cover when they left the White House. But that was a celebrity shot with credits including not just the name of the photographer but also the names of the dress designer, the hairdresser, and the makeup man.

But Gorbachev! On the cover of a magazine whose previous notion of an appropriate European cover subject was Claus von Bulow! I flipped open the issue and looked at the credit line. I didn't really expect to see a credit for makeup or hair. I guess I was hoping that I might at least see a credit for clothes design

("Trademark bulky blue overcoat by Konstantin Plosyetnikov"). I guess I was looking for some stability in a world that suddenly seemed unpredictable. The credit line mentioned only the photographer. The ground began to feel unsteady under my feet.

"You're overreacting again," my wife said. "*Vanity Fair* doesn't always have movie stars on the cover. You yourself once mentioned that they sometimes have puff cover stories on fashion designers who are in a position to buy a lot of advertising pages."

True. I had mentioned that in the course of speculating about why Ronald Lauder, a Republican fat cat whose service as ambassador to Austria was once summarized on national television by Ted Koppel as "a laughingstock," had laid out nine or ten million dollars for a hopeless run at being elected mayor of New York. (When he was asked by reporters about the appropriateness of spending that much on his own campaign, he said, "It's money I've earned." Since the Estée Lauder cosmetic empire was founded by his mother and is run by his older brother, Lauder presumably earned his fortune by not running away from home. Considering what you read now and then about the mother, that may have been no small accomplishment, but it is not normally considered a qualification for public office.)

My favorite theory had been among those put forward in the *New York Observer* by Daniel Lazare, who had also done a piece for the *Columbia Journalism Review* on how routinely *Vanity Fair* runs complimentary articles on fashion-world advertisers — including almost identically headlined covers on both Calvin Klein and his wife ("Partners in Style") and Ralph Lauren and his wife ("Pardners in Style"). In 1987, Lazare pointed out in the *Observer*, *Vanity Fair* ran an article on Ambassador Lauder that portrayed him as the sort of dynamo the Republicans should run for high elective office rather than as a, well, laughingstock. Lazare speculated that Ronald, not quite up to understanding how the article was connected to his mother's advertising, actually took it seriously.

But what was so reassuring about the possibility that *Vanity Fair* sees Gorbachev as a hot advertising prospect? What could he be intending to advertise?

"I don't like it," I said to my wife. "I don't like tinkering with the natural order of things."

"It's not tinkering with the natural order of things," my wife said. "Eastern Europe is now a very fashionable subject, and it's perfectly natural for fashion magazines to write about it."

I knew she was just trying to reassure me, but what she said made the world seem even more unpredictable. Over the years I've become accustomed to the idea that if I want to see what rich people's summer houses look like, I can just pick up a copy of *House & Garden*. "Get a load of those curtains!" I can say to my wife. "I'll bet those suckers cost a bundle. Whooee!" That's the natural order of things.

I'm not ready to see a *House & Garden* spread on Lech Walesa's apartment in Gdansk. (" 'A sort of elegant simplicity is what we're looking for,' the Walesas told trendy Kharkov interior decorator Stanislaw Kizchowski when embarking on the first redecoration since Kizchowski presided over some renovations made necessary in 1981 by the damage inflicted during a secret-police raid.")

I'm not ready for a cover of *GQ* that features one of the East German church leaders who faced down the Communists in Leipzig. I don't want to pick up *Vogue* and read what people are wearing to the trials of former members of the Securitate in Bucharest.

While I was stewing over this, my wife said she had an errand to do. When she returned, she said that she had been at the newsstand. "Jack Nicholson is on the cover of *GQ*," she said. "Just as he always is."

I looked at her suspiciously. "How about *House & Garden*?" I asked.

"A feature on the rose as 'the flower of the moment,' " she said.

"*Town and Country?*"

"Alison Eastwood," my wife said.

"Alison Eastwood?" I said. "Is that a Bulgarian name?"

"She's Clint Eastwood's daughter," my wife said.

I could feel myself relaxing.

"Are you O.K.?" my wife asked.

I nodded. Clint Eastwood's daughter was on the cover of *Town and Country*. All was right with the world.

Tamale Tension

January 29, 1990

IT TOOK THE UNITED STATES ARMY to teach us that even tamales are not innocent if they fall into the hands of the wrong person.

The wrong person in this case is, of course, General Manuel Noriega. According to the *Washington Post,* the Army has finally acknowledged that the fifty pounds of cocaine that American invasion forces discovered in one of General Noriega's hideaways turned out to be, upon closer inspection, fifty pounds of tamale flour.

You may have jumped to the conclusion that the Army is embarrassed by the discovery that it used innocent tamale flour to support its portrait of General Noriega as a cocaine-snorting scoundrel. If that's the conclusion you jumped to, the innocent party is, I'm afraid, you rather than the tamale flour.

These tamales, the Army now says, were to be used in voodoo "binding rituals." These were wicked tamales. I don't mean wicked tamales as in the phrase that might be used by a satisfied customer in some slick new margarita outlet — "Hey, these are wicked tamales!" I mean wicked tamales.

Don't be embarrassed. When I heard about all of this, I felt innocent myself. Here I was confident that I knew just about every use you could make of a tamale — eat it, throw it at the guy at the bar who made an insulting remark about your haircut, mold it into tamale art, jam it under a door end-to-end with a lot of other tamales to keep out the draft, pile it up side-to-side with thousands of tamales to save decent folks' homes from the rising waters of the Chattahoochee River — and I had never heard of using a tamale in a binding ritual. Burritos, sure. But tamales!

O.K., don't get excited. I've never actually heard of a burrito binding ritual either. I'll admit that. But at least a burrito binding ritual is possible to envision. There's a lot of sticky stuff in a burrito. I can see using a layer of refried beans and then a layer of Monterey Jack cheese, with some shredded lettuce thrown in there the way they put reinforcing rods in cement.

I suspect that's a combination that might be enough to bind together a couple of folks until help arrived with the equipment and know-how for a more permanent solution — at least if they were the sort of folks who did not object strongly to being bound together in the first place. But the same is certainly not true of tamales. I think anyone who tried a binding ritual with tamales would have a serious problem with crumbling. That's just my opinion, of course. I'm no engineer.

Speaking strictly as a layman, and as someone with very little experience in rituals of any kind, I have to say that it all sounds kind of gruesome to me. I suppose that may be the Army's intention. General Maxwell Thurman, the commander of an invasion whose mission was to bring Manuel Noriega back to this country for trial — a proper American trial in which the defendant faces an unbiased jury of his peers and is innocent until proven guilty — has gone out of his way from the start to assure us that there is no aspect of Noriega's life that is not sodden with depraved guilt. If our soldiers had found a tuna-fish sandwich in Noriega's headquarters, I suspect General Thurman would have called a press conference to hint that Noriega was not simply the sort of person who wore red long johns and owned pictures of unclad women but the sort who might well have been planning a tuna-fish sandwich binding ritual had our boys not arrived just in the nick of time.

All of that is fine for General Thurman. He has his place in history assured: the first American officer of flag rank to pause in a military operation for a discussion of the enemy commander's underwear. But how about the rest of us — particularly the rest of us who happen to be fond of tamales? Are we going to be left in permanent suspense as to what a tamale binding ritual is and how it differs from a tuna-fish sandwich binding ritual? Are we going to provoke suspicion every time we make an absolutely innocent remark like "Boy, would half a dozen tamales and a cold beer hit the spot"?

I thought I caught an odd look from the waitress when I ordered half a dozen tamales and a cold beer at our local border outpost last night. Just in case, I said, "I assure you, madam, that I have nothing untoward in mind." She nodded and walked away. "I'm just going to eat them," I shouted after her. "Otherwise, I would have ordered burritos."

Stored Away

February 12, 1990

LEARNING THAT the Defense Department may have stored away thirty billion dollars' worth of things it doesn't need made me feel a lot better about my basement.

We don't have anywhere near thirty billion dollars' worth of stuff down there. In fact, according to the lowest estimate — that would be my wife's — what we have in our basement has no monetary value at all. She didn't actually prepare a formal estimate with hard numbers; I've put them together by extrapolation from the phrase "a bunch of worthless junk."

I should say right away that the Pentagon strongly denies that its warehouses hold unneeded equipment and uniforms and supplies worth thirty billion dollars — a figure arrived at by staff members of the Senate Budget Committee. A Defense Department spokesman told a woman from the *New York Times* that the real figure is more like eight or nine billion dollars. It may be that the *Times* reporter, representing her fellow citizens, responded to that by saying, "Oh, only eight or nine billion — well, not to worry, then." And it may be that she didn't.

Actually, the Pentagon wouldn't exactly say that the supplies in question are unneeded. What the Defense Department calls this stuff is "inapplicable inventory." It's a phrase I'm sorry I didn't know years ago, when my mother was always after me to clean up my room.

"I want this pigpen you live in straightened up right now!" she'd say. "And I mean it."

"I shall endeavor to dispose of the inapplicable inventory at my earliest possible convenience," I could have said.

"I'll apply something to you in a minute, young man!"

My wife has the same attitude toward the basement that my mother once had toward my room at home: there's a lot there she'd just as soon see in the trash. I'm afraid she has the sort of attitude that makes you understand why this country is running out of places for solid waste disposal.

On the other hand, I feel sure that if the Pentagon had ever had my wife on its staff it wouldn't have found itself in this embarrassing predicament. When Senator Jim Sasser, the chairman of the Senate Budget Committee, said his people had "constructively directed attention to some of the problems in the system," he expressed, in a nicely senatorial way, precisely the policy my wife has adopted toward the need to straighten out the basement. Around our house, we call it nagging.

"You're really going to have to do something about the basement," my wife said, for instance, on the very day the story about the extent of the Pentagon's inapplicable inventory came out. By coincidence, it also happened to be the day after the man who reads the gas meter had lost his way in our basement. He had wandered around down there for three or four hours before I ran across him while checking, out of idle curiosity, to see if we still had that broken fourteen-inch black-and-white television I once stored somewhere, just in case.

"Oh, the basement's not so bad," I told my wife. By chance, I had just been reading about some of the supplies the Army had tucked away over the years and then forgotten. "At least we don't have 215,000 female dress shirts in 126 sizes down there," I told my wife. "At least we don't have 150,000 pairs of Korean War–vintage cold-weather pants or a thirteen-thousand-year supply of a machine tool used to make circuits for the F-14 fighter plane."

"What makes you so sure?" she said.

Actually, I was pretty sure we didn't have a thirteen-thousand-year supply of anything — something that could not have been said categorically of the house I grew up in. When my mother ran across a particularly worthwhile sale, she could not resist buying in large lots. As a math exercise in junior high school, I once calculated that we had a three-thousand-year supply of baking soda and enough Tabasco sauce to last us, at our normal rate of consumption, until the year 3814.

My wife had been talking a lot about what could have happened to the meter reader if I hadn't gone down to check for the black-and-white TV — which, by the way, might be behind that old bookcase that's jammed in a corner in a way that makes it impossible to move and might not be. I tried to put the incident into perspective ("The man simply had no sense of direction"), but she insisted we were facing a crisis. Finally I agreed to look in the Yellow Pages for some sort of hauling company.

"Sorry," I reported after some study of the larger ads. "There are some places here that do trash, but it says nothing at all about inapplicable inventory."

Obvious Appointment

March 5, 1990

NATURALLY, IT WAS MY FRIEND Wayne Marshall who spotted the small item in the *New York Times* reporting that the president of Exxon's shipping subsidiary, Frank Iarossi, resigned to become chairman of a standards-setting organization for the shipping trade. Wayne sent over the clip under the heading "Ironies Beyond the Capacity of Any Writer to Invent."

Wayne goes in for that sort of thing. He also collects ugly postcards. Don't send him one of those jackalope postcards that people are always sending from Wyoming or someplace. Wayne could paper his house with jackalope postcards. He says people whose idea of an ugly postcard is a jackalope postcard have a paucity of imagination. Wayne does not have a paucity of imagination himself. I've been through the collection, and I can attest that Wayne has got some ugly postcards.

The sort of newspaper item Wayne likes to tell me about is the sort that will almost invariably draw the response "You've got to be kidding!" It wasn't Wayne who drew my attention to the item about someone's inventing designer trash bags or the item about how the fifty pounds of cocaine the Army said it found in Manuel Noriega's quarters turned out to be tamale flour, but those were his kind of stories.

Wayne and I both like to imagine the scene that might have taken place, say, between the two American Army officers in charge of reporting all the wicked stuff found at General Noriega's house. "Maybe we should have it tested before we say definitely it's cocaine, sir," says Captain Richard Gonzales, of El Paso, Texas.

"What else do you think it could be, captain?" says Lieutenant Colonel Darrell (Buzz) Barton, a man who cultivates his reputation in the regiment for biting sarcasm, as he signs the order for the press conference. "Tamale flour?"

I've grown to depend on Wayne for drawing my attention to such newsworthy items as the recent career good fortune of Frank Iarossi. It turns out that a remarkable number of such items appear in the business section, and I gave up reading the business section a long time ago — even before it started looking suspiciously like the police blotter. Too many numbers. I figured Wayne was always around to flag me if something interesting popped up. If the phone rang tomorrow and it was Wayne telling me that Ivan Boesky had just been made chairman of a Wall Street commission to establish ethical standards for traders or that Robert Campeau was going to teach a course at Harvard Business School on how to take over department store chains or that the Savings and Loan Institute had named Charles Keating chairman of its senatorial relations committee, it wouldn't surprise me. Of course, I'd say, "You've got to be kidding!" — I wouldn't want to disappoint Wayne — but it wouldn't surprise me.

I told Wayne it was interesting that Iarossi's appointment as chairman of the American Bureau of Shipping was announced just after Exxon ships managed to have two oil spills off New Jersey in the same week; it was also just a couple of days after a federal grand jury in Alaska indicted Exxon on two felonies and three misdemeanors connected with the eleven million gallons of oil that the *Exxon Valdez* spilled in Prince William Sound while Iarossi was in charge. This guy sounds like he has such a predilection for spilling oil that he might be considered a menace in a self-service filling station. ("Oh, don't trouble yourself with the hose, Mr. Iarossi — a big executive like you. LeRoy'll be right out to get you whatever you need.")

"Then let's make him manager of an organization that sets standards for the shipping industry," Wayne said, in a merry tone of voice. I hadn't seen him so cheerful since an aunt of his sent him a color postcard of a monument in eastern Pennsylvania honoring the inventor of asphalt siding. "Then we can be sure that the standards on oil spills will be pretty exacting: No more than eleven million gallons in any one sound or harbor. No more than two spills a week of any size."

I knew that Wayne could see the American Bureau of Shipping's board of managers sitting around a polished mahogany table, trying to select a chairman. One member is still reluctant ("Are you sure we can't get the *Exxon Valdez* skipper himself?"), but the others have been thoroughly convinced by Iarossi's curriculum vitae and a nice letter of recommendation from the CEO of Exxon and some dramatic color pictures of oil-covered birds on Alaska beaches. Color pictures! Did Wayne have another interest in this? I don't think so. Those pictures would make postcards too ugly even for Wayne's collection.

The Marriage Business

March 12, 1990

IT HAS FINALLY DAWNED ON ME that my wife and I got married during that awkward period in the history of domestic relations between dowries and prenuptial agreements. It's embarrassing enough these days to be involved in a long-term marriage — an institution, I acknowledged some time ago, that is strongly identified in the public mind with the music of Lawrence Welk. Now it turns out that we're involved in a long-term marriage that is without benefit of sensible business planning.

Although I am certainly correct in stating that there was no dowry involved, I should, just for the record, take note of the fact that my wife did bring a large console radio to the marriage. On the other hand, it was broken. It cost $37.50 to repair. Not that anyone's counting. The figure just happened to stick in my mind. In terms of the bridal payments of cattle practiced in some African tribal societies, you might say that the radio amounted to a payment of a couple of cows, one of which had a touch of hoof-and-mouth disease.

I myself had furniture amounting to a red Victorian couch of surpassing beauty and elegance — a couch I loved even though it conjured up in my mind the late-nineteenth-century segregated railroad car that figured in Plessy *v.* Ferguson, the case that established for some years the principle of separate but equal accommodations in the South. I thought the Victorian couch went rather well with the broken radio, although my wife did not agree. We sold the couch. Marriage, as they say, is compromise.

I figure I missed a dowry by two generations. My grandfather — who immigrated to Kansas from a part of Europe that changed hands so often he claimed to have deserted three separate armies — told me that the sum mentioned to him by my grandmother's brothers was $500. He also told me that they never forked over the money. Apparently, the thought of returning my grandmother for nonpayment never occurred to my grandfather. He was a kindly man.

Sixty years or so later, when my wife and I decided to tie the knot, there was no mention at all of business arrangements, except, of course, for my father's customary inquiry as to the condition of my intended's teeth. My father often startled young and romantic men by his response to their news of having at last found the girl of their dreams. "How are her teeth?" he always said. He had the strong feeling that although handicaps of looks or intelligence or background could be dealt with, bad teeth caused a permanent financial drain that could wreck a marriage.

A dowry hadn't occurred to us, and I'm not certain that we were aware of the existence of prenuptial agreements — except maybe in the case of some ninety-two-year-old millionaire who had fallen hard for his manicurist. If someone had suggested that we draw up a prenuptial agreement, we might have said that it wasn't necessary to go to all that trouble: if things didn't work out, my wife would take her radio, I would take my couch, and she, of course, would leave with the teeth she came in with.

My new awareness of prenuptial agreements comes from the noisy break-up of the noisy Trumps — an episode, it seems to me, that is the equivalent of a circus turned ugly, with the clowns in the little car trying to run each other over and the lion finally getting an opportunity to chomp an ear or two off the trainer. I can't claim to have followed the battle in detail, but what did stick with me from the coverage was the realization that my wife and I were without an agreement of any kind. Theoretically, she could walk out of this marriage with my American Hereford Association Poster. Even worse, she could insist that I take the cat. I realized that I was, at least technically, in what the lawyers call an exposed position.

On the other hand, I think of some advice my mother often gave: Why start something? The radio is working fine. If we just don't say anything, maybe everyone will assume that we're the sort of sophisticated people who routinely update our prenuptial agreement every year on our wedding anniversary. I think we can just go along the way we've been going, keeping our little secret. I just hope nobody tells Liz Smith.

The End, Maybe

March 19, 1990

RECENTLY, I DECIDED that talk about the new decade had become so maddeningly ubiquitous (". . . and so if the pet food industry is to be successful in meeting the challenges of the '90s . . .") that I was not going to burden the public with my observation that cholesterol counts are the miles-per-gallon of the '90s. Now, just when I was beginning to have some hope that '90s talk was dying down, a dispute has begun to develop over what event constituted the symbolic end of the '80s. When it comes to observations on the culture, there's no rest for the weary.

Oddly enough, this issue seemed all but settled as early as the summer of 1989. All the commentators appeared to agree that the symbolic end of a decade known for conspicuous consumption came when Malcolm Forbes, the late Laird of Loot, flew a couple of planeloads of big shots and glitz-hounds and bootlickers and (most important of all) advertisers to Morocco for a two-million-dollar birthday party. In its obituary of Forbes, *Newsweek* repeated that the party in Morocco "will probably be remembered by historians as the swan song of the entire ostentatious decade."

Fine. I was always willing to give Malcolm Forbes the benefit of the doubt myself. Given the field of high-profile showing off — a field that may have enjoyed its golden age in the past ten years — watching Forbes somehow always seemed sort of entertaining, while watching Donald Trump just made you want to shudder. I'm not certain exactly why, although it could have been because Forbes, unlike Trump, gave the impression of understanding it was all a joke. In terms of Hollywood adventure movies, the difference between Forbes and Trump was the difference between Harrison Ford and Sylvester Stallone.

In fact, I always liked to think that whatever Forbes did was done partly as a prank — a device not simply for promoting his magazine while getting some kicks but for keeping the pot bubbling, preferably while a few people wearing tuxedos were bobbing around in it. It occurred to me more than once that, considering his penchant for motorcycles and hot-air balloons and boats, Forbes had, in the guise of entertaining rich and mighty fun-lovers, scared the wits out of a lot of them and given a bad case of seasickness to a lot of others. I sometimes used to think of Forbes hard at work at his desk, trying to see if, with all of his imagination and all of his resources, he could design a glitzy event so palpably silly that even Henry Kissinger and Barbara Walters wouldn't show up. I could imagine him thinking, on a slow morning, "Maybe I should select six hundred people who would kill to be included in a gathering of the very important, fly them over to Morocco in August, and imprison them in a hotel that doesn't have air-conditioning." So it was all right with me if they wanted to call his party the end of the '80s.

I liked the idea of the whole thing ending with a lot of people sweating through very expensive clothing.

Then Drexel Burnham Lambert went belly-up. A lot of decade analysts said that, since the '80s were known for greed and maniacal money-fiddling, the collapse of the firm that invented junk bonds, following not that long after both the firm and its premier junkist were visited by federal prosecutors, had to be the symbolic end. Other people said that the true symbolic end was the discovery that just before Drexel executives said there was no money in the till they had managed to find $195 million for their own bonuses. That was an act, some observers argued, that was obviously the ultimate example of the sort of behavior that will someday be described as "very '80s."

But then the analysts who interpret the '80s mostly in terms of its ostentation countered with the Trump split-up as the end of the decade. Other analysts, maintaining that the Trump split-up was simply the continuation of the '80s in a slightly different tone of voice, said maybe the real end was American Express's firing of Shearson Lehman Hutton's chief executive, a relentless money-grubber identified in the *New York Times* headline as "Symbol of '80s Boom," along with hundreds of other Shearson employees — including, I devoutly hope, every single person who phoned me around dinnertime and, referring to me cheerfully by my first name, told me what a splendid investment opportunity had come to the attention of good old Shearson Lehman that very day.

"I've never known you to take any pleasure in someone being out of a job," my wife said when I expressed that hope out loud.

She's right, of course. It may be that I was not unaffected by the past ten years myself. Maybe we should stop arguing about how it ended and simply hope that it's really over.

Afterword

I THINK this would be the proper place to acknowledge any errors I might have made in the foregoing pieces. I do not include outright lies in this category. Those you're going to have to find for yourself.

I want to thank readers who have been so conscientious about writing to me to point out errors or state disagreements — although I'd like to say to Mrs. D.B. of Canton, Ohio, that fair-minded people should be able to disagree without the use of such words as "dingbat" and "meathead."

It would be gratifying to report that most of the letters I receive from readers are about subjects like deficit reduction and the future of the Atlantic alliance. As it happens, though, most of them are about fruitcake. I'm not saying that I get no mail at all on national issues. A number of readers, I have to report, believe me to be insufficiently appreciative of the subtleties of Dan Quayle's mind. They occasionally send me letters expressing that thought in spirited phrases like "probably not as dumb as all that."

Also, I still get mail about the Gipper — actually, about my contention some years ago that I had found the real George

Gipp (as opposed to the one in the movie, played by Ronald Reagan) in a nursing home in Lodi, New Jersey, occupying his sunset years by stiff-arming nurses' aides and telling anyone who would listen that he went to Notre Dame only because he couldn't get into Holy Cross. Even at this late date, I hear from readers who claim to have read an article in the *Reader's Digest* saying that the real Gipp actually died while he was at Notre Dame, just the way the movie said he did. I have a sort of form postcard to deal with those letters: "Who are you going to believe, the *Reader's Digest* or me? It's not even a full-size magazine."

But most of my mail is about the fruitcake question. I've never exactly kept that a secret, although I won't claim that I blurt it out when one of my colleagues fixes me with a profound look and says, "Getting much mail on the future of the Atlantic alliance?"

"Not much" is what I say. He doesn't need to know that I've never actually received a letter about the future of the Atlantic alliance. He doesn't need to know that I've never actually written anything about the future of the Atlantic alliance. "Not much" will do him just fine.

Also, in talking with my colleagues I see no reason to bring up the fruitcake question. I suppose I could try my own profound look — which, I regret to say, strikes most people as the sort of expression you might find on someone who has just eaten a piece of particularly dreadful fruitcake — and say, "Getting much mail on the fruitcake question?" I don't. I don't mention the Gipper, either. Sometimes, if I've just received an eloquent and heartfelt letter from a supporter of the Vice President, I might say, "Getting much mail that says he's probably not all that dumb?" They never are.

I should also point out, more or less in my defense, that some of the things I've said in columns were not meant to be taken as absolutely factual. In that category I would include a statement in my coverage of the Iowa caucus campaign, when the people running for President sounded like candidates for appointment as extension agent of the south-central agricultural planning district. I would like to say in the most direct possible way that Michael Dukakis was never under the impression that you have to kill a cow to get the cheese. That was meant as a little joke.

Yes, I realize that it would be a lot less complicated simply to label little jokes. But it would also be a lot less underhanded, and I have my reputation to think of. For those whose letters indicate that they see nothing at all strange about the proposition that you have to kill a cow to get the cheese, by the way, all I can say is that you ought to think about getting out a little more.

Do I get ideas from readers? I always expect to. I always expect to open a letter and read some tip couched cleverly in the form of an innocent question, like "Does it occur to you, when February rolls around and we start hearing about Black History Month, that they gave the black people the shortest month?" Or "If Lincoln freed the slaves and preserved the Union, how come 'Lincolnesque' just means tall?" Or "When did historians begin referring to the second term of the Reagan Administration as Voodoo II?"

I don't get many of those. Instead, I get mostly letters about fruitcake. Some readers say that whoever told me that there is only one fruitcake that is simply passed along from person to person at Christmas was wrong, because they have been in a room with two fruitcakes at the same time. Even more readers say that I couldn't be right about nobody's ever having bought a fruitcake to eat himself, since they have purchased many fruitcakes for themselves — although receipts are never enclosed. Some readers take my side on the fruitcake issue. R.G.M. of Mankato, Minnesota, for instance, says it has been scientifically proven that fruitcake is literally indigestible ("It's like having a brass doorknob in your stomach"), so that if people really did eat fruitcake there would eventually be no room left for anything else and they would starve to death.

Although I didn't have the heart to say this to R.G.M. after all the research he did — he even found a detective novel in which the medical examiner says to the investigating detective, "I would say that the victim had dinner four to six hours before he was murdered, and it's certain that within the last fifteen or twenty years he ate two pieces of fruitcake" — I would just as soon drop the entire matter. It's sort of a vicious cycle: readers write me about fruitcake and so I answer their questions about fruitcake and that draws more letters about fruitcake.

What harm does that do? Well, for one thing, it leaves little room for discussion of the future of the Atlantic alliance. Also, let's say that a new acquaintance who has been told that I write a newspaper column — we can call the new acquaintance Norbert — begins to ask me for advice to the lovelorn and tips on Certificates of Deposit in an attempt to find out what sort of column I write. Someone else wanders over and says to Norbert, "You mean you don't recognize the name?"

Norbert, looking rather sheepish, shakes his head. I am looking rather pleased myself.

"Well, I'm surprised to hear that," the newcomer says. Then he introduces me as Calvin Trillin, the noted fruitcake columnist.